RESEARCH HIGHLIGHTS IN SOCIAL WORK 42

Reparation and Victim-Focused Social Work

Research Highlights in Social Work

This topical series examines areas of particular interest to those in social and community work and related fields. Each book draws together different aspects of the subject, highlighting relevant research and drawing out implications for policy and practice. The project is under the editorial direction of Professor Joyce Lishman, Head of the School of Applied Social Studies at the Robert Gordon University.

Risk Assessment in Social Care and Social Work
Edited by Phyllida Parsloe
ISBN 1 85302 689 1
Research Highlights in Social Work 36

The Changing Role of Social Care
Edited by Bob Hudson
ISBN 1 85302 752 9
Research Highlights in Social Work 37

Mental Health and Social Work
Edited by Marion Ulas and Anne Connor
ISBN 1 85302 302 7
Research Highlights in Social Work 28

Adult Day Services and Social Inclusion
Better Days
Edited by Chris Clark
ISBN 1 85302 887 8
Research Highlights in Social Work 39

Transition and Change in the Lives of People with Intellectual Disabilities
Edited by David May
ISBN 1 85302 863 0
Research Highlights in Social Work 38

Social Care and Housing
Edited by Ian Shaw, Susan Lambert and Daniel Clapham
ISBN 1 85302 437 6
Research Highlights in Social Work 32

Performance Review and Quality in Social Care
Edited by Anne Connor and Stewart Black
ISBN 1 85302 017 6

RESEARCH HIGHLIGHTS IN SOCIAL WORK 42

Reparation and Victim-Focused Social Work

Edited by Brian Williams

Jessica Kingsley Publishers
London and Philadelphia

All rights reserved. No paragraph of this publication may be reproduced, copied or transmitted save with written permission or in accordance with the provisions of the Copyright Act 1956 (as amended), or under the terms of any licence permitting limited copying issued by the Copyright Licensing Agency, 33–34 Alfred Place, London WC1E 7DP. Any person who does any unauthorised act in relation to this publication may be liable to criminal prosecution and civil claims for damages.

The right of the contributors to be identified as authors of this work has been asserted by them in accordance with the Copyright, Designs and Patents Act 1988.

First published in the United Kingdom in 2002 by
Jessica Kingsley Publishers Ltd
116 Pentonville Road
London N1 9JB, England
and
325 Chestnut Street
Philadelphia, PA 19106, U S A
www.jkp.com

Copyright © 2002 Robert Gordon University, Research Highlights Advisory Group, School of Applied Social Studies

Library of Congress Cataloging in Publication Data
A CIP catalog record for this book is available from the Library of Congress

British Library Cataloguing in Publication Data
A CIP catalogue record for this book is available from the British Library

ISBN 1 84310 023 1

Printed and Bound in Great Britain by
Athenaeum Press, Gateshead, Tyne and Wear

CONTENTS

I.

Introduction

Brian Williams

Reparation by offenders to the victims of crime has undergone a spectacular revival in the United Kingdom since the late 1990s, but the new policies governing its use have not always been informed by research. Similarly, the social and probation services and youth offending teams have had to undertake increasing amounts of work with the victims of crime, often prompted by new legislation, but staff awareness of issues relating to victimisation has lagged behind, at a time when new initiatives are being introduced with great frequency and speed. Here again, the findings of relevant research have much to offer both policy-makers and practitioners, although they have not necessarily been directly drawn upon in devising policy or in designing new programmes in practice.

Research on work with victims of crime is reported in an unusually wide range of journals, and the researchers involved in it straddle a variety of disciplines including sociology, criminology, social work and law. That range is reflected among the contributors to this collection, and in the chapters themselves, but the book brings a summary of much of this material together in one place with a view to making it more accessible to practitioners. The chapters both summarise relevant research and describe what has been found to be effective practice. The contributors include experts in their academic fields and experienced practitioners who have contributed significantly to the developments described.

In England and Wales, an adversarial legal system has tended, at least until recently, to assume that victims of crime have no legitimate interest in the outcome of criminal trials. There has been considerable suspicion, on the part of judges and lawyers, about involving victims in the legal process. For example, anyone who might have to give evidence at a trial has to be regarded as a potential witness, and there are strict rules about the extent to which witnesses, including the victim, can discuss an offence with other people. This has meant that many victims have been advised not to seek therapeutic help in dealing with the consequences of a crime until after the trial is over, for fear that their evidence would be 'contaminated'. Until recently, this has prevented victims of serious crime from receiving immediate help which could have speeded their recovery (and might have improved their ability to give cogent evidence). Although this issue has recently been addressed in Home Office and Crown Prosecution Service guidance, which sets out the circumstances in which witnesses can receive pre-trial help, it illustrates the traditional marginality of victims in the criminal process (CPS 2001; Williams, forthcoming).

Even where the legitimate interest of victims is recognised, staff in the criminal justice system do not always find it easy to understand or accommodate victims' needs. Recent legislation has changed the role of victims in the criminal process, but this has been done without changing the fundamental nature of that process. For example, the victim personal statement represents an attempt to incorporate a victim's perspective, not previously available to the courts, but the new arrangements introduce an extra possibility of victims being drawn into the adversarial process. If they are made aware of the possibility that they may be cross-examined about contested aspects of the statement, victims may be reluctant to participate. Perhaps victims' evidence should not be privileged, and defendants do need to be protected from the danger of arbitrary sentencing based on the circumstances of individual victims (see Walklate, Chapter 9). But the victim statement is an example of a 'pro-victim' initiative which has been tacked on to the existing adversarial system without such conflicts being resolved.

Greater clarity is needed about the circumstances in which victims should be, and wish to be, directly involved in the response to crime, and those in which they would prefer to forfeit decision-making to a third party (see Wemmers, Chapter 3). It has been suggested that victim statements may have primarily a cathartic effect, recognising the losses suffered by victims without necessarily influencing sentencing decisions (Rock 1998). If so, the distinction made by Wemmers between bilateral and third-party decision-making has important implications for practice.

In a similar way, the family group conference, itself an adaptation of a Maori traditional method of doing justice, has been incorporated into the youth justice system in New Zealand and adapted for use elsewhere. In its original context, it represented a distinct and free-standing model of dealing with offending. It was then adapted for use in the white colonial criminal justice system in New Zealand, at first alongside an adversarial approach, but it subsequently largely replaced the adversarial system there (at least in relation to young offenders). In the most recent stage of its journey, conferencing has been grafted onto a punitive adversarial youth justice system in England and Wales, where it sits rather uncomfortably alongside the range of community and custodial penalties already available to the courts. In the process, the centrality of the victim's concerns is in danger of being lost. The new system is operated by multi-agency youth offending teams, and although in many cases it will be a police officer who makes contact with the victim to discuss their possible involvement in the conferencing process, victims would perhaps be justified in feeling that the process is offender- rather than victim-centred. The research on the pilot projects and on restorative cautioning schemes suggests that such concerns are justified (see Dignan 1999; Masters, Chapter 4).

Reparation by offenders to their victims, or symbolically to the wider community, has received a great boost from the introduction of reparation orders in the youth justice system in England and Wales since the implementation of the Crime and Disorder Act of 1998. However, the new orders raise a number of ethical and practical issues for youth justice practitioners, which are discussed in detail by Dignan in Chapter 5. The introduction of compulsion (for offenders but not for victims) makes the new provision in England and Wales particularly problematic, and it will be interesting to see whether this proves to be a continuing issue once the new orders are in routine use (Williams 2001).

Dignan's research is part of a wide-ranging evaluation of the new youth offending teams introduced in England and Wales in 2000. It has influenced the development of reparation within the teams by its timely identification of some of the practical and theoretical difficulties with the pilot projects. It has also helped to demonstrate the benefits of basing policy upon empirical evidence – although the government did not go so far as to await the findings of the pilot evaluations before implementing the planned changes! Nevertheless, the commitment to rigorous evaluation of new criminal justice projects is welcome and long overdue.

As general awareness of the needs of victims of crime increases, so the particular issues raised by specific types of crime become more prominent. The decision to order a public inquiry into the investigation of the racist murder of Stephen Lawrence had far-reaching consequences not only for policing, but for all agencies involved in working with victims and survivors. For the first time, the government had deliberately taken steps to 'inject race and racism into the politics of victims' (Rock 1999, p.22). The inquiry report pointed not only to an urgent need to tackle institutional racism in the way these agencies operate, but also to ensure that all racially motivated crime is taken seriously and that victims are thus encouraged to come forward. To achieve this, a programme of staff training in victim awareness and effective responses will be required, as well as effective inter-agency working. Once reporting rates improve (as they have, dramatically, in London since the establishment of the Metropolitan Police Racial and Violent Crime Task Force in 1998), effective action needs to be taken by all the agencies with a part to play (see Chouhan and Knight, Chapter 7). This will clearly include the probation and social services, youth offending teams and victim support agencies as well as the police.

The concept of 'hate crimes' is new to the UK and does not fit easily with an individualised approach to criminal justice. Racial and other forms of aggravating factors have long been taken into account in sentencing, but it is a recent innovation to legislate for such an approach. It appears from American research that hate-motivated crime can have a significantly greater impact upon victims than, for example, other types of vandalism or harassment (Laurence 1999). This is beginning to be recognised in inter-agency crime prevention work, and by the police. Not only is racially motivated crime increasingly prioritised, but so are homophobic assaults and harassment. There is, as yet, much less awareness of other types of hate crime, although the North American literature covers homophobic crime and crime motivated by disability discrimination (Conley *et al.* 1992; Sobsey 1994) and there is a growing awareness of the latter issue elsewhere (Carmody 1991; Sanders *et al.* 1997). In the UK, it is an aggravating factor if an offender chooses a victim specifically because they are vulnerable by reason of infirmity or extreme old age, but the law does not seem to recognise discrimination on the grounds of disability, nor on the grounds of sexual orientation. The insights arising from implementing the Stephen Lawrence inquiry report seem likely to include an understanding that discrimination on the grounds of age, sexuality, disability and culture is as unacceptable within the criminal justice system and elsewhere as racial and sexual discrimination. This will create new challenges for all the criminal justice agencies, including the voluntary victim assistance groups.

Criminal justice responses to male violence within the home have improved as awareness of gender inequalities has increased since the 1970s. Few agencies, however, have had sufficient resources to enable them to work effectively both with offenders and with their victims. As Morran, Andrew and Macrae show in Chapter 11, agency responses to women victims of male violence have traditionally been ambivalent at best, and at worst they have colluded with offenders' rationalisations and denial. Scottish courts and social workers have pioneered more effective responses which hold men responsible, and the research evidence summarised in this part of the book shows how effective a properly resourced, victim-focused response to 'domestic' violence can be. Criminal justice systems around the world (with some exceptions[1]) are beginning to put their recognition of the needs and rights of victims of crime into effect by introducing state-funded compensation for the victims of violent crime. The spread of such compensation schemes illustrates the growing role of supra-national bodies, such as the European Union, in criminal justice policy-making, as Goodey shows in Chapter 2. The research shows that European compensation schemes have an important symbolic role as well as their practical purpose. The wide differences between the arrangements in the countries of Europe also illustrate the challenges involved in any attempt to harmonise social policies in this way, not least because of the enormous philosophical variations underlying different criminal justice systems.

There are also enormous differences between services for victims in urban and rural areas. Drawing upon her own research in Scotland, Moody (Chapter 6) illustrates the nature and extent of the problem of providing flexible and appropriate services to victims of crime in rural areas, and demonstrates the need for further research in this area. Criminology has traditionally neglected the rural element, and this chapter helps to redress the balance.

Several contributors to this volume refer to the cultural change involved in convincing criminal justice professionals of the benefits of recognising and meeting the needs of victims of crime (Tudor, Dignan, Dominey, Masters). The experience of the probation service in England and Wales, suddenly faced with important new responsibilities in respect of victims of crime under the Victim's Charter, is instructive. Despite ethical misgivings and serious resource constraints, probation officers managed to devise professional ways of helping victims of serious crime, and in the process the organisation as a whole developed a more balanced approach to working with victims and offenders (Williams 1999; Johnston 1997). This was not achieved easily or without conflict, as Tudor shows (Chapter 8). Nevertheless, it was a significant achievement, and one which should encourage those who seek to create a more victim-friendly and victim-focused youth justice system. One of the lessons of the probation experience was that practitioners need time to absorb paradigm shifts of this kind, and that in-service training can provide opportunities for reflection and re-focusing. Too much staff training attempts to impose an orthodoxy, rather than stimulating debate about professional ethics. Workers who have trained and committed themselves to working with offenders need to be shown the potential advantages of engaging with victims, and for many it is unwelcome and frightening. A little more sensitivity to these dynamics might have made the introduction of youth offending teams less traumatic and disruptive (Bailey and Williams 2000).

Within the probation service, work with victims has changed from a minority interest to an increasingly central part of the rationale and role of the service. As Tudor's chapter shows, research has had an important part to play in that process. As in the case of rural victims, however, there are huge under-researched areas in relation to victims of crime. Tudor points to some of the gaps, and so does Jane Dominey's chapter in this volume. Despite the widely-held belief that offenders' demonstration of remorse and empathy for their victims predicts improved future behaviour, there is little if any empirical evidence to back this assumption. This is rather disturbing, given the role of assessments of these characteristics both in sentencing and in decision-making about early release from prison. Making the best of the available knowledge and drawing upon practical experience, Dominey indicates how knowledge of the impact of offences upon victims can be used to inform such assessments.

A recurrent theme in many of the chapters in this volume is the rapidity of change in criminal justice, particularly in relation to victims of crime. At the time of writing (March 2001) the government has just published its proposals for a revised, third version of the Victim's Charter (Home Office 2001). These suggest that radical change is again on its way. Before long, victims could be given much wider statutory rights, and it is likely that a victims' ombudsman will be created. All the recommendations of the European Union's 1999 framework decision on basic rights for victims of crime are about to be implemented, and the shortcomings of the 1996 Victim's Charter will mostly be rectified. For the first time, government funding will be provided for some radical, victims' self-help organisations, including Rape Crisis (Social Work Alliance 2001). The Charter provisions in relation to the victims of sentenced offenders will be extended wherever possible to victims of acts by mentally disordered offenders subsequently sent to secure hospitals. The responsibilities of the Crown Prosecution and police services (pre-trial) and the probation service (post-sentence) in relation to keeping victims informed will be enormously increased (see Tudor, Chapter 8). The pace of change does not seem likely to diminish in the foreseeable future.

In the face of such rapid change, we hope that this collection will provide practitioners with an overview of the research they need to know about in order to practice effectively.

Note

1. For example, South Africa, where compensation to victims of crimes of violence has not been introduced because of the likely cost, but limited arrangements for compensation in the case of property crimes have been in place for some time.

References

Bailey R. and Williams B. (2000) *Inter-agency Partnerships in Youth Justice: Implementing the Crime and Disorder Act 1998*. Sheffield: Social Service Monographs.

Conley R.W., Luckasson R. and Bouthilet G.N. (eds.) (1992) *The Criminal Justice System and Mental Retardation: Defendants and Victims*. Baltimore: Brookes.

Crown Prosecution Service (2001) *Provision of Therapy for Child Witnesses Prior to a Criminal Trial: Practice Guidance*. London: CPS Communications Branch.

Dignan J. (1999) 'The Crime and Disorder Act and the prospects for restorative justice.' *Criminal Law Review,* January, 48–60.

Home Office (2001) *A Review of the Victim's Charter*. London: Home Office. (Also at http://www.homeoffice.gov.uk/cpd/revitch.pdf)

Johnston P. (1997) 'Throughcare practice, risk and contact with victims.' In H. Kemshall and J. Pritchard (eds.) *Good Practice in Risk Assessment and Risk Management 2*. London: Jessica Kingsley Publishers.

Laurence, F.M. (1999) *Punishing Hate: Bias Crimes Under American Law*. London: Harvard University Press.

Rock P. (1998) *After Homicide: Practical and Political Responses to Bereavement*. Oxford: Clarendon.

Rock, P. (1999) 'Current developments in policy-making for victims in England and Wales.' In Home Office Special Conferences Unit conference report, *The Role of Victims in the Criminal Justice Process.* London: Home Office.

Sanders A., Creaton J., Bird, S. and Weber, L. (1997) *Victims with Learning Disabilities: Negotiating the Criminal Justice System.* Oxford: University of Oxford Centre for Criminological Research.

Social Work Alliance (2001) 'Government seeks views on victims' bill of rights.' socialworkalliance email newsgroup, 27 February.

Williams B. (1999) *Working with Victims of Crime: Policies, Politics and Practice.* London: Jessica Kingsley Publishers.

Williams B. (2001) 'Reparation orders for young offenders: coerced apologies?' *Relational Justice Bulletin* 9, January.

Williams B. (forthcoming) 'Counselling in legal settings: provision for jury members, vulnerable witnesses and victims of crime.' In P. Jenkins (ed.) *Legal Issues in Counselling and Psychotherapy.* London: Sage.

2.

Compensating Victims of Violent Crime in the European Union

The Case for State Restitution

Jo Goodey

Introducing state compensation

> ...it is usually futile for courts to award heavy damages for personal injuries; the isolated individual offender can rarely make large amends. What, then, could be done to provide the compensation which the victim ought to receive? (Fry 1959, p.192)

Margery Fry's short but influential article on the desirability of state compensation for victims of violent crime was a significant milestone in the historical development of state compensation schemes. Today, state compensation to victims of violent crime is a well-established means of victim restitution in a number of common law jurisdictions. In light of recent initiatives to introduce state compensation schemes for victims of violent crime across the European Union (EU), this chapter critically explores the role of state compensation alongside existing alternatives which attempt to obtain restitution for victims from offenders. State compensation is offered as a prime example of the current push for harmonisation of victim-centred justice, across the EU, against a background of divergent forms of victim-centred provision in different EU jurisdictions. Taking Fry's point that individual offenders are often unable to pay compensation to their victims, alongside the argument that the state ought to take some responsibility for its 'occasional failure to protect' (Fry 1959, p.193), the political motives behind these recent EU developments will be reviewed without losing sight of the likely benefits of state compensation for victims of violent crime.

The chapter begins by examining the motives behind the introduction of state compensation schemes. Case studies of state compensation in three different EU member states (Britain, France and Italy), alongside alternative means of victim compensation, are outlined. The chapter concludes with a brief critical overview of state compensation as a form of victim restitution, as currently promoted at the level of the European Union.

Critical readings of state compensation

In his 1978 book *Responses to Victimisation*, David Miers argued that political factors were the 'single most important determinant behind the introduction of victim compensation schemes' (Miers 1978, p.51). Miers rejected the suggestion that state compensation was an altruistic 'Good Samaritan' act by the state on behalf of victims. Rather, he proposed that state compensation primarily affords political credibility to those who introduce and administer a scheme. To believe that state compensation schemes are initiated with the sole purpose of 'helping' victims of crime, by awarding state compensation as a form of public restitution to victims, is to deny the political reality of much victim-centred work in an era when governments need to be seen to be doing something about crime. This may appear as a jaded response to state compensation but, in light of evidence from research by Burns (1980) and Shapland (1984), this would appear to be the case with respect to early compensation schemes in North America. However, in the case of Britain and other European countries, Shapland is more positive about the motives behind the introduction of state compensation, which she sees as grounded in humanitarian and social welfare ideals of equitable justice and reciprocity in social relationships.

Burns (1980) outlines key rationales for the justification of state compensation schemes. These include the 'legal duty' of the state to compensate crime victims because, in its failure to prevent crime, society creates criminals and cannot ensure restitution from the offender to the victim. This 'legal duty' rationale, if applied in practice, would be impossible to administer, given the scale of crime. In comparison, the 'moral duty' argument, whereby the state is justified in helping victims on humanitarian and welfare grounds, which are not a given right, is generally preferred by governments as a less expensive option. Following on from the 'moral duty' rationale, state compensation can also be viewed as a form of 'loss distribution' along the lines of social insurance. In this case it is argued that as crime is unavoidable, society should share the cost of insuring against social harm. Those who are most likely to be victims of crime are also the least able to pay an insurance premium, and, therefore, should not be held personally responsible for insuring their own safety. These rationales are additional to the 'benefit to the state' argument which sees the introduction of state compensation as a means of ensuring that justice appears to be done in order to promote the interests of the state.

In outlining these rationales, one must not forget to ask what victims of violent crime actually need and want by way of financial restitution, while acknowledging that some victims may not need or want compensation from either an offender or the state. In those countries and individual cases where financial provision for pain and suffering and/or loss of earnings may come from other sources, such as the welfare state and insurance premiums, payment of compensation from either an offender or the state may be superfluous to a victim's financial requirements. Similarly, as compensation payments tend to come some time after an offence or a trial, be these payments in a lump sum or in instalments, they can serve to remind victims of a painful incident they would rather forget. Ultimately, financial restitution to victims, from offender or state, should be an act of restitution; as Shapland's research with 278 adult victims of violent crime confirmed, compensation, from whatever source, was generally regarded by victims as 'giving back or recompensing to the victim what he [sic] has lost, not only materially but symbolically and in terms of suffering' (Shapland 1984, p.145). In Shapland's research, compensation was regarded by victims as more than an act of charity.

In the long term, when state compensation schemes pay mere lip-service to victims' actual needs and are not grounded in distribution of 'real' funds, then, as a form of restitution, they are likely to be a dismal failure for both state and victims. Alternatively, if a scheme originally instigated for political reasons goes on to administer and distribute significant financial funds successfully, then should criticism really take the moral high ground, if one takes into account the limited ability of offenders to pay restitution orders, or the demands imposed on a victim who has to initiate their own civil claim for compensation? On the other hand, if victims still like to receive compensation from offenders, state compensation should not be introduced as a wholesale solution to the problems of obtaining financial restitution from offenders, as victims might consider state compensation as a secondary form of restitution.

Over-arching these considerations is the question of how far a state compensation scheme fits the nature and goals of the existing criminal justice system with regard to victims and, where they exist, the state's welfare provisions. It is interesting to note the extent to which state compensation schemes have been initiated in common law jurisdictions with strong welfare traditions which already cater for the health and income needs of citizens. As the case of Britain illustrates, introduction of state compensation appears, on first glance, to be bolted on to state welfarism. In this tradition, the way state compensation is distributed to recipients can be viewed critically as a socially divisive mechanism for sorting the 'deserving' from the 'undeserving' poor in the absence of provision for the victim to claim compensation directly from the offender in the course of a criminal trial. With these criticisms in mind, the following paragraphs review the provision of compensation in Britain, from state and offender, prior to comparing the British experience with continental European practice.

Compensation in Britain

In 1964 Britain was the first country in Europe to introduce a system of state compensation for victims of violent crime[1]. The administration of the British scheme, involving the assessment of applications and the payment of money, was undertaken by the then Criminal Injuries Compensation Board (CICB). Victims apply directly to the scheme for compensation, or through an intermediary if their age or some other reason necessitates help in filling in the forms, and await the outcome of the application, which can, if necessary, be challenged. Victims should, unless there are mitigating circumstances, submit their application for compensation within two years of the violent act.

It took two decades before the British scheme was finally put on a statutory footing, and in 1995 the Criminal Injuries Compensation Act was passed. In force since 1 April 1996, the Act compensates victims of violent crime for: (1) personal pain and suffering; (2) loss of earnings; (3) costs of care. Most significantly, the Act introduced a controversial tariff-system of awards which, in 2001, ranges from a minimum award of £1000 at level 1, for an injury causing, for example, blurred or double vision lasting 6 to 13 weeks, through to a maximum award of £250,000 at level 25, for paralysis of all four limbs[2]. On the introduction of the Act, the CICB was replaced by the Criminal Injuries Compensation Authority (CICA) which was given the task of administering the new tariff system. At present, the CICA receives around 80,000 claims for compensation a year and has, in recent years, paid out an average of £200 million per annum in compensation[3].

Britain's early enthusiasm for state compensation can be partially attributed to the pioneering work of criminal justice reformers like Margery Fry, which was taken up by the government of the time[4]. The apparent need for state compensation can only be understood in the context of a common law system which does not afford the victim a ready means of claiming compensation from an offender. In comparison, the continental or inquisitorial system of law, as practised elsewhere in Europe, provides the victim, at least in theory, with the opportunity to act as a civil claimant of compensation during the criminal trial – something which a British victim is unable to pursue. Also, British state compensation has to be understood as part of the country's postwar welfarist tradition, which ascribed to the state a duty to provide for citizens' needs; however, in the case of criminal injuries compensation, this duty was, and is, not a given right.

In turn, this welfarist tradition of state provision merged in the 1970s with calls from feminist and other grass-roots organisations for increased recognition of, and provision of services for, vulnerable victims. At the same time, Britain's Victim Support network, today a nation-wide government-aided organisation which assists over one million victims each year, began in Bristol. However, while Victim Support has grown, presenting the acceptable face of victim-centred initiatives in Britain, other movements, with more radical origins, such as Rape Crisis and women's refuges, have not been as fortunate in obtaining and sustaining government funding in the scrabble for scarce resources (Mawby and Walklate 1994). With this background in mind, state compensation to victims of violent crime needs to be read as part of the conforming and acceptable face of government-funded victim assistance in Britain.

From its origins in 1964, the CICA has reiterated two central points when outlining an applicant's eligibility to receive compensation: first, the applicant must have been injured as a result of a crime of violence; and second, the applicant must be an 'innocent victim'. The idea of the 'innocent victim' is central to the CICA's remit. People with significant criminal records and with unspent convictions, or those whose conduct is considered as influencing their own victimisation, are either excluded from receiving compensation or may have their awards reduced on the basis of the CICA's scale of penalty points. The main justification for this prioritisation of certain victims over others is that public funds are being utilised, and therefore must be spent wisely in order to evoke 'public sympathy' for the injured victim. While this may appear to be a sensible way of ensuring that public funds, as a finite resource, go to the 'right' people and, as far as possible, that fraudulent claims are avoided, this needs to be set against the fact that many victims of violent crime will be excluded from state compensation. This is particularly the case for certain demographic and socio-economic groups which are likely to experience high levels of offending and victimisation, such as young men, and those whose social situation and conduct may place them in the category of 'undeserving' victim – for example, a woman working as a prostitute, or a young man who is drunk at the time of an offence against him.

The alternative in Britain to state compensation for victims of violent crime is the award, by a criminal court, of a compensation order from the offender to the victim as part of a penal sanction. Unlike on the continent, the victim does not have the right to make representations to a criminal court for the award of compensation; this is undertaken by the Crown Prosecution Service (CPS), which represents the victim. The state, on behalf of the victim, also has the responsibility to collect compensation from the offender upon the award of a compensation order; this is undertaken through the magistrates' court (even when compensation is awarded by a crown court). Non-payment of a compensation order can result in a custodial sentence for the offender.

The compensation order was first introduced in England and Wales under the 1972 Criminal Justice Act. Under the Act, a sentencer could order an offender to pay compensation to their victim with regard to any loss, damage or injury incurred by the victim, whilst having due regard to the financial means of the offender. Ten years later, the 1982 Criminal Justice Act recognised the need to prioritise the offender's payment of compensation to the victim before any payment of a fine to the state. In the case of impoverished offenders, the 1982 Act stipulated that compensation orders could form the sole basis of a sentence. While the developments for victims under these two Acts appear laudable, the reality of practice proved that sentencers were slow to prioritise compensation orders over fines. Also, in cases of personal injury, sentencers were unsure of the appropriate sum to award for various injuries.

In 1988, the government attempted to rectify the situation through a series of reforms. First, a guideline on compensation awards, drawn up by the CICB, was distributed to the criminal courts. Second, the 1988 Criminal

Justice Act stipulated that the courts had to give reasons for not awarding a compensation order in cases where there was an identifiable victim who was eligible for compensation. Third, Home Office Circular 20/1988 gave the police the duty to ensure that all relevant information about the injuries and losses suffered by a victim were passed on to the CPS as part of the case file which would inform the court.

It might appear, in the light of the above, that significant developments have been made in recent years in the award of compensation orders as part of a sentence. Maguire and Shapland's research (1990) certainly confirms that victims are keen to receive compensation from offenders as a form of direct restitution. However, their research also indicates that victim dissatisfaction sets in when a compensation award is thought to be too little, when the courts fail to inform victims of the amount due and the means being taken for enforcement of payment, and, perhaps most importantly, when victims are not informed of reasons for non-payment. The same complaints arise with respect to the administration and award of state compensation. Most discouragingly, as evidenced by Moxon's (1993) research on magistrates' courts, courts continue to neglect their duty to give reasons for not awarding a compensation order. Here, the law in the books does not match the exercise of the law in practice. Recognition of a victim's need for information regarding the progress of a compensation order or the award of state compensation is essential (Wemmers 1996).

While compensation orders might provide an alternative to state compensation for victims of violent crime, they are limited to cases where a known offender can be found and convicted; herein lies the advantage of state compensation, which does not need to identify an offender. The compensation order does not assist those victims whose offender is not charged with an offence. In such cases the victim might be eligible for state compensation but, given the minimum tariff, which is currently set at £1000, this tends to exclude those whose injuries are considered to be minor. In turn, this appears to discriminate against the needs of some of the most vulnerable and socially deprived victims of crime who might benefit from a payment that falls below the minimum tariff set in 1996. In the CICA's search for the 'innocent' victim, the distinctions drawn up between the 'deserving' and 'undeserving' victim of crime would appear to impact negatively on some of those most in need of restitution from the state.

Bearing in mind the above criticisms of state compensation, it must be acknowledged that the British scheme, under the CICA, is the most advanced and, consequently, the most expensive compensation scheme currently in existence in the EU. The following paragraphs present a brief critical overview of some of the alternative methods by which a victim of violent crime might obtain financial restitution elsewhere in the EU.

Compensation in France

In 1998 the varied array of victim support services in France, most of which were set up in the 1980s under the direction of local prosecutors, received 15 million francs from the Ministry of Justice. In the same year, state compensation funds received more than 800 million francs in funding (Brienen and Hoegen 2000, p.310). While state compensation has enjoyed a long history of government support in France, in comparison with some other EU member states, victim support schemes, because of their privately initiated nature, have not been as fortunate in gaining the support and the profile they deserve. The National Institute for Victim Support and Mediation (INAVEM), established in 1986, was founded as an umbrella organisation to provide support to the range of private victim programmes across France, and has been increasingly successful in drawing together the disparate interests of these victim services. In France, the emphasis on victim assistance remains with state compensation to victims of crime, despite the fact that localised victim support services supply victims with invaluable information about the criminal justice process, which includes advice on obtaining compensation from the state.

State compensation for victims of crime was first introduced in France in 1977. A series of state funds have been set up over the years to assist victims of crime and other disasters, including a fund for people with AIDS

(Lombard 1996). The 1990 state fund for victims of serious crime and sexual offences was combined, through the Reform Act of July 1990, with the 1977 fund for victims of crime, to extend the coverage of the 1977 provision (Wergens 1999). The committee which oversees the state funds is known as CIVI (Commission d'Indemnisation des Victimes d'Infractions). All applications for an award should be received by CIVI within three years of the violent act. However, the application process is not free, and applicants generally apply for legal aid to assist them with a claim. Brienen and Hoegen (2000), in their overview of victim services in France, reiterate the comments of most French specialists in praising CIVI's work as the most progressive victim-centred initiative in France since the 1980s; however, when compared with the British average of 80,000 applications per year, the number applying for state compensation in France – 10,865 in 1997 (see Brienen and Hoegen 2000, p.316) – seems paltry.

The main alternative in France to state compensation for victims of violent crime is the *partie civile* or adhesion model, which, in theory, affords the victim a great deal of power. Under the *partie civile* model the victim can enjoy an active role, as a civil claimant, in both instigating and taking part in a criminal trial, in order to claim compensation from the offender. Compensation, awarded in the course of a criminal trial, remains part of civil law in France, and is generally awarded in addition to a penal sanction.

There are three central problems with the French *partie civile* model: first, compensation from the offender to the victim does not have priority over the payment of a fine to the state; second, in the court's obligation to award compensation covering the full range of costs incurred by the victim, the victim is very unlikely to receive the majority of the award, given most offenders' inability to pay; and third, the victim is left with the responsibility of wresting their compensation from an offender via the bailiffs. In comparison, CIVI, the state compensation committee, receives co-operation from the criminal justice authorities in locating offenders for the purpose of reinstating money, paid by the state to victims, back into government funds. While there have been a number of initiatives by the French government to make the seizure of offenders' assets on behalf of victims easier, these have generally been regarded as being of little success (Brienen and Hoegen 2000, p.337)[5].

While the *partie civile* model may seem like a victim-centred idea in theory, because the victim can apparently take control of their own compensation claim from the offender, in practice, the principle tends to be a dismal failure with respect to the sums recovered. The failure of the *partie civile* model helps explain the growth of, and enthusiasm for, state-funded victim compensation in France, which might be negatively attributed to an attempt by the French government simply to be seen to be doing something for victims. However, given the range of state funds for a series of traumatic events that go beyond a limited reading of the 'criminal', it would seem that the French treatment of victims comes under a welfarist tradition of state responsibility and humanitarian assistance, coupled with a healthy growth, since the 1980s, in victim support services. In view of this, Italy provides a neat example of limited responses to victims in a context where the state is mistrusted as the guardian of citizens' needs and rights.

Compensation in Italy

In Italy, there is no general state compensation scheme for victims of violent crime (Wergens 1999). However, provision does exist to compensate victims of terrorism and organised crime, under the 1990 Act, nr.302. Under this Act, state compensation is payable for certain injuries arising from an act of terrorism or the actions of the 'mafia'. Injuries which are eligible for compensation must cause permanent disability which reduces the victim's capacity to work by 25 per cent or more. The sum of the award is established on the basis of an incremental scale, with the maximum payment being in the range of 150 million lira for total disability. Family members and dependants of a deceased victim can claim compensation under the terms of the Act (Brienen and Hoegen 2000, p.521). A compensation board assesses applications, which, as with the British system, should be received within two years of the injury or death[6].

The above provisions, under the 1990 Act, reflect the limited remit of the Italian state when it comes to helping a wide range of victims of violent crime, and victims in general. The Act is not a measure of the government's willingness to assist the victim of crime, but is illustrative of the Italian state's particular problems with organised crime and acts of terrorism[7]. Once again, the state must be seen to be doing something for victims; but, in the case of Italy, this tends to be of a limited nature.

The victim of violent crime has one alternative avenue open, should he or she wish to pursue a claim for compensation. As in France, the victim can act as an aggrieved party to criminal proceedings in order to make a compensation claim. A civil claim against the accused, in the form of a statement by the victim, can be added to the criminal proceedings. The primary civil consequences of an offence, once a defendant has been found guilty, are: (1) payment of damages to the victim; and (2) reimbursement of maintenance expenses incurred by the state. This second form of restitution obliges the offender to reimburse the state for up to two-thirds of the maintenance expenses he or she has incurred while in prison. These two forms of restitution, to the state and the victim, are in conflict with each other, and, ultimately, this cannot be in the victim's interests. Also, much like the pre–1982 situation in England and Wales, which saw the prioritisation of a fine paid to the state over the award of compensation to the victim, the situation of the Italian victim is not enhanced by the fact that compensation cannot substitute a penal sanction in Italy.

While the Italian civil claimant, as part of the criminal proceedings, can request that the court enforce a provisional compensation payment to the victim, the bulk of claims for compensation, if awarded, are generally referred by the criminal court for settlement at a civil court (Piva 1996). Here the age-old division between criminal and civil courts comes into play, as Italian criminal judges, mirroring their British and French counterparts, feel more at ease when the two systems of law are kept apart. This works against the best interests of victims, particularly given the dire state of the Italian civil courts, where cases take an average of eight to ten years to conclude (Brienen and Hoegen 2000, p.532). The courts, having agreed on an award of compensation, do not provide the victim with assistance in the collection of the sum owed. As in France, victims have to pay for their own bailiffs to retrieve their money. Once again, as exemplified by the Italian state's pursuit of money owed to it by the offender for incarceration in a state penal institution, the state puts its own financial needs before those of victims[8].

The Italian victim's limited options for the award and receipt of compensation from the state or an offender, either as a result of a violent act or some other personal loss, are not the only area where the victim may feel at a loss. In general, Italian victims suffer from a lack of service provision when compared with the situation of victims in a number of other EU jurisdictions, for example: Britain; the Netherlands; Sweden. No national victim support organisation exists in Italy. Instead, there are a number of local services, mostly based in the north of the country, which target particular victim groups and are politically active in lobbying government with respect to their own agendas. This pattern of single interest victim lobbying is atypical of most EU victim service providers which, when they exist, tend to establish a relationship with governments that is to their mutual benefit in securing victim funds and assisting victims (INAVEM in France and Victim Support in Britain).

Research by Savona (1993), conducted in 1992, tellingly reveals that 44 per cent of Italian victims claim to receive no help from any source, while 38.3 per cent get help from family, friends and the local community, 14.1 per cent receive some assistance from the police, and a mere 4 per cent obtain assistance from social welfare organisations – 0.5 per cent of which collectively constitute victim support services and voluntary organisations. What this research confirms is two things: first, the lack of adequate victim assistance and service provision in Italy; and second, the deep distrust in which Italians hold the state. The fact that over 40 per cent of victims received no assistance from any source does not tell us whether they actually wanted assistance; however, there appears to be a vacuum of victim assistance which family and close acquaintances are readily filling in the absence of adequate help from the police and social services. Victim assistance, as illustrated by the poor state of victim compensation, is not a priority of the Italian state. While the state wants to be seen to be doing something about Italy's most pressing crime problems, organised crime and terrorism, it is evident that the full range of victims' needs and rights is not of paramount importance to the Italian criminal justice system. The 1988 Code of Criminal Procedure, which radically reformed the Italian criminal justice system, went some way, in theory, towards enhancing the rights of the victim in criminal procedure; but, as with the theoretical rights of the *partie civile* in France, theory has not been met in practice, particularly in the area of compensation. Given the continuing problems of much of the Italian criminal justice system, from long delays in court through to corruption at the highest levels, it is perhaps unsurprising that victims come low down on the system's 'list' of reforms.

Moves for state compensation across the EU

Focusing on state compensation to victims of violent crime, and given the examples of compensation to victims in Britain, France and Italy, there are several moves afoot, at the level of the European Union, to rectify the situation across the EU with respect to unequal provision of compensation to victims.

In 1983 the Council of Europe signed the European Convention on the Compensation of Victims of Violent Crime. While the Council of Europe's conventions are not legally binding for the European Union, the Council's human rights agenda sets the tone for a number of EU initiatives. The 1983 Convention on State Compensation has fed into the 1998 action plan of the Council of the European Union and the European Commission on how best to implement the provisions of the Treaty of Amsterdam on an Area of Freedom, Security and Justice within the EU. Point 51 of the action plan focuses on compensation schemes and the need for a comparative study of existing schemes in the EU. The inclusion of this point was a significant step towards ratification of the 1983 Convention at EU level and, in due course, moves towards co-operation and ultimate harmonisation of state compensation schemes across the EU.

The importance of state victim compensation is further referenced in the European Commission's 1999 communication to the European Parliament, the Council of the European Union, and the Economic and Social Committee: 'Crime Victims in the EU: Reflections on Standards and Action'[9]. This communication fed into the discussions at the EU summit in Tampere, which set out to further the objectives of the Amsterdam Treaty, and was given a mandate in the Tampere conclusions (32), which included victims' right to compensation and the need for national programmes to provide assistance to victims. More recently, on 11 August 2000, the Council of the European Union made direct reference (in its 'Draft Framework Decision on the Standing of Victims in Criminal Procedure') to the action plan and, in particular, Point 51 on the issue of victim compensation schemes.

In October 2000 practical steps were made at an expert group meeting in Sweden[10], on 'Compensation to Crime Victims in the European Union', to push the mandates of the action plan and Tampere. To this end, having already undertaken a comparative study of state compensation schemes in the EU[11], the Swedish organisers of the expert meeting called on the European Commission to elaborate upon the recommendations of the meeting in a Green Paper which would further initiatives on state victim compensation at the level of binding legislation across the EU.

Concluding thoughts

The above testifies to the fact that state compensation to victims of violent crime can no longer be ignored by individual member states of the Union, such as Italy, which do not make sufficient provision for all victims of violent crime. While the *partie civile* model, favoured in a number of European Union jurisdictions, appears to offer the victim a means of obtaining compensation from the offender, in reality it offers the victim more false hope than promise. Given the resistance of many criminal judges and prosecutors to the place of a civil claim for compensation in a criminal trial, and the marginal number of victims who are successful in obtaining compensation from offenders through this process, the only real alternative for victims of violent crime would appear to be state compensation.

Whether the good intentions of the European Commission to ratify state compensation legally in the EU will result in substantive changes in a number of member states, has yet to be seen. As the early criticisms of Miers (1978) and Burns (1980) revealed, it is easier for states to legislate and express their good intentions towards state compensation without realising actual changes on the ground which result in payments to victims in need.

Certain questions served to tax the deliberations of the expert group meeting in Sweden, particularly those points which examined the rights of EU citizens to receive compensation from another EU member state in which they were victimised. In consideration of this, it was agreed that victims should claim compensation from the state in which they were victimised, but they could receive the assistance of their normal state of residence when applying for compensation. Here, the question of different rates of victim compensation in different member states needs to be more thoroughly aired; and, in turn, the question of how each member state would fund a compensation scheme which, given the case of Britain, could rapidly grow in popularity given adequate promotion.

Ultimately, in taking state compensation as the current example of moves towards harmonisation of standards of service provision for victims of crime in the EU, one must look beyond the political rhetoric to judge the feasibility of any binding legislation. While it might be the case that Italy and Greece[12], along with all the other member states, may ratify any forthcoming legislation on state compensation schemes for victims of violent crime, this does not mean that they will adhere to the terms of the legislation beyond the instigation of a scheme with limited and poorly advertised funds. Given that the expert meeting in Sweden concluded that compensation to the victim should be sought primarily through the offender, with state funds as a fallback, one must return to question the motives of the EU's latest push for state compensation schemes. In that alternatives to obtain compensation from the offender have largely proved to be a difficult process across the EU, state compensation might appear as a practical solution to a real problem. However, alongside the action plan's calls for a comparative study of compensation schemes in the EU, there should have been calls for a comparative study of victims' needs and wishes concerning the desirability of compensation orders from offenders alongside alternative means of obtaining financial restitution.

Whether the latest EU moves for state victim compensation simply allow the Union to be seen to be doing something for victims has yet to be determined. Promotion and possible harmonisation of state compensation in the EU needs to establish a clear rationale as to why this is desirable: first, for victims, and second, for the EU and its individual member states with their very different histories and priorities concerning criminal justice provision. The latest EU position papers can be read in the line of 'moral duty' to victims as 'innocent' EU citizens in need of state assistance, but in reality they could prove to be mere political posturing which serves to exclude certain victims, those least desirable victims, from state assistance. The test of the EU's convictions will lie with the future extent and successful award of compensation to a satisfied range of victims of violent crime across the EU.

Notes

1. New Zealand, in 1963, was the first country to legislate for state compensation, under the 1963 New Zealand Criminal Injuries Compensation Act (No.134). In 1972 New Zealand went on to introduce the Accident Compensation Act (No.43), thereby ensuring that victims of violent crimes and other 'accidents' were covered under New Zealand's compensation legislation.
2. See CICA website: http://www.cica.gov.uk
3. Information presented by the deputy director of the CICA at an expert group meeting on compensation to victims of crime in the European Union, held in Umeå, Sweden, 23–24 October 2000.
4. In 1960, Schafer published *Restitution to Victims of Crime*, a report for the Home Office, the conclusions of which were reported in the document *Compensation of Victims of Criminal Offences* (1974) 10 Crim L Bull 605.
5. In the case of dismissals, some of which may include acts of violence, the public prosecutor has two other avenues open to try and obtain compensation for the victim: (1) the case can go to mediation with the aim of securing compensation from the offender to the victim; (2) a conditional dismissal can be made on the understanding that the offender pay compensation to the victim.
6. Unusually under the terms of Act, provisional sums of money, awarded prior to any final decision on compensation by the responsible committee, do not have to be returned to the state if no compensation is forthcoming.

7.   The legislative and criminal justice emphasis on organised crime can also be seen with regard to Italy's use of witness protection for vulnerable and at-risk victims, which is primarily aimed at witnesses and informants in organised crime cases.

8.   Should the offender receive a suspended sentence or parole, no importance is assigned by the court to the civil damages which the victim might claim from the offender; these lesser charges effectively lessen the victim's eligibility to claim compensation from the offender.

9.   Brussels, 14.07.1999, COM(1999) 349 final.

10.   The meeting was held in Umeå, Sweden, 23–24 October 2000, and was hosted by the Swedish Crime Victim Compensation and Support Authority (a government body supported by the EU's Grotius programme). The author attended the meeting as a rapporteur.

11.   To be made public in 2001.

12.   Italy and Greece, alone among EU member states, have no general state compensation scheme.

References

Brienen M. and Hoegen E. (2000) *Victims of Crime in 22 European Criminal Justice Systems.* Nijmegen: WLP.

Burns P. (1980) *Criminal Injuries Compensation.* Toronto: Butterworth.

Fry, M. (1959) 'Justice for victims.' *Journal of Public Law* 8, 191–194.

Lombard F. (1996) 'France'. In D. Greer (ed.) *Compensating Crime Victims: A European Survey.* Freiburg-im-Breisgau: Max-Planck-Institut, 227–247.

Maguire M. and Shapland J. (1990) 'The "Victims Movement" in Europe.' In A.J. Lurigio, W.G. Skogan and R.C. Davis (eds.) *Victims of Crime: Problems, Policies and Programs.* London: Sage, 205–225.

Mawby R. and Walklate S. (1994) *Critical Victimology.* London: Sage.

Miers D. (1978) *Responses to Victimisation.* Abingdon: Professional Books.

Moxon D. (1993) 'Use of compensation orders in magistrates' courts'. *Research Bulletin 25.* London: Home Office.

Piva P. (1996) 'Italy'. In D. Greer (ed.) *Compensating Crime Victims: A European Survey.* Freiburg-im-Breisgau: Max-Planck-Institut, 373–400.

Savona E. (1993) *Experiences, Fear and Attitudes of Victims of Crime in Italy.* Rome: UNICRI, No.49.

Shapland J. (1984) 'Victims, the criminal justice system and compensation.' *British Journal of Criminology* 24, 2, 131–149.

Wemmers J. (1996) *Victims in the Criminal Justice System.* Amsterdam: Kugler.

Wergens A. (1999) *Crime Victims in the European Union.* Umeå: The Swedish Crime Victim Compensation and Support Authority.

3.

Restorative Justice

The Choice between Bilateral Decision-making Power and Third Party Intervention

Jo-Anne Wemmers

Introduction

In recent years we have seen increasing support for restorative justice and with it a growth in the development of extrajudicial measures such as mediation, victim–offender reconciliation programmes and family group conferencing. In these programmes interested parties, typically victims and their offenders, are brought together in order to find a mutually satisfying response to the crime. Often, such a response will include restitution. While a third party may act as a mediator facilitating the process, the decision-making power typically remains with the two parties who have the power to accept or reject any proposal made by the mediator.

Some scholars, such as Roach (1999), consider the fact that the victim maintains decision-making power to be an important advantage and argument in favour of extrajudicial measures such as mediation. According to Christie (1977), is his now classic article on conflict as property, the criminal justice system 'robs' parties of 'their' conflict. Christie argues that victims should have the *right* to their own conflict. Extrajudicial measures leave the conflict and its resolution with its original 'owners', namely, the victim and offender. The traditional criminal justice process does not allow the victim to play an active role in the decision-making process. Christie (1977) claims that victims of crime have lost their rights to participate.

Initiatives to enhance the role of victims in the traditional justice system have been met with resistance (Wemmers 1994; Groenhuijsen 1999; Roach 1999). As the ongoing debate on victim impact statements shows, merely allowing victims to have input – not even decision-making power – at sentencing is a highly controversial step (see Kelly and Erez 1997). Consequently, the criminal justice system has been slow to acknowledge victims of crime.

In contrast to the conservatism of the criminal justice system, extrajudicial measures are more flexible. This is because they are not bound by the same legal restrictions as judicial measures. The role of victims can be moulded to fit the goals and the organisation of the particular programme.

Some supporters of restorative justice go so far as to suggest that the restorative justice paradigm should replace the traditional criminal justice paradigm, and speak of a 'paradigm shift'. For example, Weitekamp (1999) argues that the old traditional criminal justice system does not work any more and that we are currently witnessing a shift towards restorative justice. Similarly, Roach (1999) argues that the traditional criminal justice system neglects victims' rights; moreover, in the few instances where it includes victims' rights, it does so only when this coincides with its own interests, namely, crime control. Restorative justice is seen as a more satisfying alternative for victims of crime.

While extrajudicial measures may be attractive for legal scholars looking to find a simple way to include the victim in the justice process, it is not clear whether or not they are an attractive option for victims. After all, restorative justice was not developed by victim advocates but by those working with offenders. An important question in this respect is whether or not victims actually want decision-making power. Do victims want to determine the outcome (sentence) of their case or are they happy to leave decision-making to the legal authorities? In this paper I will examine theory and research regarding decision-making procedures and the implications for victims of crime. The central question in this paper is: under what conditions should victims prefer to keep decision-making power (bilateral decision-making power) and when should they prefer to forfeit decision-making power to a third party? The paper closes with policy recommendations for restorative justice programs.

Procedural justice

Procedural justice is a body of theory and research regarding the perceived fairness of procedures, first developed in the seventies by Thibaut and Walker (1975), whose early work on procedural justice focused largely on dispute resolution procedures such as legal procedures. One of the questions examined by Thibaut and Walker (1975) is when disputants will turn to a third party (for example, a mediator or a judge) to help them resolve their conflict, and how much power they are willing to give to a third party. The research is relevant because it provides indicators regarding the types of procedures that parties (victims and offenders) should prefer and, in particular, how much control parties should want to retain.

According to Thibaut and Walker, people are motivated by self-interest and therefore seek to obtain and maintain control over decisions that might affect their outcomes (Thibaut and Walker 1975; Lind and Tyler 1988). At the same time, however, people recognise that the maintenance of social relationships and the resolution of disputes sometimes require that control over decisions be relinquished to a third party. Thibaut and Walker distinguish two types of control: process control and decision control (Houlden *et al.* 1978). Process control refers to the extent to which parties can decide what information is presented during the dispute resolution hearing – in other words, it reflects whether or not parties are allowed any input into the process. Decision control refers to the extent to which parties are free to reject or accept the result of a third-party intervention – in other words, how much control parties have over the outcome. According to Thibaut and Walker (1975), parties are willing to forfeit decision-control provided they retain process control.

In two of their studies, Thibaut and Walker examine the conditions under which parties desire third-party intervention in disputes and the forms of third-party intervention that appear best to meet the desires of disputants. In one study (Thibaut and Walker 1975; Chapter 3) the research focused on whether disputes could be resolved by mediation. Mediation was defined as a procedure in which an impartial third party offers suggestions for resolving the dispute but does not have decision-making power. They hypothesised that mediation would be less successful in resolving disputes in which the desired outcomes of the two sides were strongly 'noncorrespondent', that is, disputes in which the two sides have opposing interests. Such cases are considered 'unmanageable' as each side wants to win and one side's gain is the other's loss. An example would be a case where the victim wants the the offender to pay a hefty sum in damages and the offender does not want to pay any damages. According to Thibaut and Walker, mediation would be unsuccessful in such cases, and parties would want a third party to have decision-making power. Correspondent outcomes, on the other hand, are outcomes where both sides share common interests or goals. For example, an offender dearly wants to avoid a custodial sanction and will gladly pay restitution to the victim in order to reach this goal, while the victim wants restitution and is not interested in seeing the offender go to prison (realising this would hinder repayment). Thibaut and Walker (1975) hypothesised that mediation would be most successful when outcomes were correspondent.

In a controlled experiment, law students participated in a simulation of mediation procedures modelled on those used in pre-trial settlement conferences. Half of the subjects attempted to negotiate a settlement for a dispute in which the potential outcomes of the two sides were mildly noncorrespondent[1]. The remaining subjects attempted to negotiate a settlement for a dispute in which the outcomes of the two sides were severely noncorrespondent. The results supported the hypothesis that subjects were significantly more likely to reach an agreement when the outcomes were only mildly noncorrespondent than when they were strongly noncorrespondent. When the two sides had opposing interests, as is the case in many real-world disputes, mediation was unsuccessful and both sides preferred giving decision-making power to a third party.

In a later study, Thibaut and Walker and their colleagues studied reactions to four third-party dispute-resolution procedures (Thibaut and Walker 1975; Chapter 2):

- mediation: where a third party may only suggest how the dispute might be resolved

- moot: where both disputants and the third party must all agree on the resolution

- arbitration: where the third party resolves the dispute by binding judgement but only after the disputants have had a chance to explain their positions

- autocratic adjudication: where the third party resolves the dispute by binding judgement without allowing parties to provide input.

These four procedures were compared to bargaining without the aid of a third party (bilateral decision-making).

These conditions can readily be translated into real-world concepts. The fourth condition, adjudication, is similar, at least from the victim's perspective, to the traditional criminal justice process. A judge (third party) takes a decision on a case without allowing the victim an opportunity to explain his/her position. An offender who is represented by a lawyer may similarly not have a chance to explain his/her position to the judge; however, one could successfully argue that this is the role of his/her counsel. Mediation is similar to many restorative justice programs where interested parties negotiate a settlement which is satisfactory to all those involved (see for example victim–offender reconciliation: Pate 1990; Wemmers and Van Hecke 1992). Arbitration is similar to programmes such as sentencing circles, where decision-making power is vested in a third party but all those involved are given an opportunity to voice their position (see Stuart 1996).

In the 1975 study law students rated the four procedures on the extent to which each procedure was desirable. A complicated weighing scheme was used to compute how well each procedure met the desires of the disputants in each condition. The results provide insight into which procedures disputants should prefer.

Overall, the results of the study showed that the arbitration procedure best met the disputants' desires for a dispute resolution procedure. This was followed by moot, mediation, bargaining and autocratic adjudication (in that order). However, under conditions of severe non-correspondence of outcomes, ideal procedures are more likely to involve high levels of third-party control. The research showed a curvilinear relationship between third- party control and desirability: parties seem to desire some third-party control but do not want too much third-party control either. Specifically, parties appear to be quite willing to forfeit decision-making power to a third party, but they want to maintain some input into the process. In the words of Thibaut and Walker (1975), process control is more important than decision control.

Research

Although based on legal procedures, the research by Thibaut and Walker does not specifically deal with victims and offenders. Instead, their studies focus on conflicts between equal parties, such as those found in civil law. The question is whether or not their findings are generalisable to other settings. Criminal cases are different from civil cases, and it may be that Thibaut and Walker's findings do not apply to criminal justice procedures. On the other hand, victims are generally not legal scholars and the distinction between criminal and civil cases may not be relevant for them. It may well be that individuals – be they parties in a civil dispute or a criminal case – place similar demands on the process.

Unfortunately, a direct test of Thibaut and Walker's work on the desirability of third-party intervention that includes victims of crime has not (yet) been conducted. There are, however, various studies which, although indirect, would seem to suggest that Thibaut and Walker's findings should also apply to victims of crime.

Wemmers (1996), for example, examined the meaning of procedural justice for victims of crime. This study, which was based on interviews with

435 victims of crime in the Netherlands, included indicators of process and decision control. As in other research on procedural justice (see for example Lind and Tyler 1988; Tyler 1990) decision control was operationalised as the amount of influence respondents felt they had on the decision of the public prosecutor. Process control was defined as feeling that one had been given an opportunity to express one's views.

The results of this study show that process control is strongly correlated with victims' judgements of how fairly they were treated (r = 0.5; p.01), while the correlation between decision control and procedural justice is much smaller (r = 0.27; p.05). In other words, for victims of crime, having the opportunity to express one's views is more important for their sense of fairness than having influence over the outcome of their case. It would seem that Thibaut and Walker's claim that of the two types of control, process control is more important, applies equally to victims of crime.

Several studies support the finding that victims place great importance on being given the opportunity to express their views. For example, in a British study, Shapland, Willmore and Duff (1985) report that victims of violent crime wish to be consulted throughout the criminal justice process and want to be informed of the developments in their case. Similarly, in his study on the preferred role of victims in the criminal justice system in Germany, Kilchling (1995) finds that victims feel that their role at both the investigation and trial stages should go beyond that of mere witness. These studies suggest that victims want to be included in the criminal justice process, and this may be viewed as the desire to maintain process control.

On the other hand, Erez and Tontodonato (1992) found that victims who are given the opportunity to express their views in a victim impact statement are often dissatisfied with the outcome. They suggest that giving victims an opportunity to express their views raises their expectations, which leads to disappointment for victims if they perceive their statement has had no influence on the outcome. This study seems to suggest that victims do want to influence the outcome or decision in their case, and that process control is just a means to that end. However, it is not clear from this study whether the respondents wanted decision-making power, or simply wanted their views to be taken into consideration by the decision-maker.

Several studies suggest that while victims do want to be consulted, they do not want decision-making power. For example, in the above study by Shapland *et al.* (1985) the authors found that most victims did not wish to play a more active decision-making role in the present court system. Similarly, in a Dutch study based on interviews with victims of serious violent crime and property crime, the author reported that 75 per cent of the respondents agreed with the statement that the victim should always be invited to attend the trial. Yet 62 per cent did not believe that the victim should have a say in the sentence, and almost half of the respondents agreed that during the trial the sentencing of the offender should receive more attention than the position of the victim (Smale 1980).

Finally, Thibaut and Walker do not suggest that parties will never want decision-making power, or that they will never want to participate in programmes like mediation. Instead they specify the conditions under which parties will choose to retain decision-making power. Specifically, when parties share correspondent outcomes, mediation will be successful. In other words, when victims and offenders share common goals, mediation will be successful. Support for this hypothesis is found in Wemmers and Van Hecke's (1992) evaluation of a Dutch mediation project called Dading. They examined the factors related to successful negotiations between victims and offenders. They conclude that the attitude of parties is an important factor. When parties are willing and able to find common ground, negotiations will be successful; when, on the other hand, the interests of both parties are opposite to one another and there is little to no common ground between them, negotiations will be unsuccessful. In the former situation (outcome correspondence) parties should prefer mediation, and in the latter case (outcome non-correspondence) they should prefer third-party intervention.

Discussion/conclusion

Overall, the victimological research supports Thibaut and Walker's contention that process control is important. Like parties in a civil dispute, victims of crime place great value on being included in the process. Accordingly, procedures that exclude victims, like the traditional criminal justice process, should therefore not be very satisfying to them; victims should prefer procedures that afford them some input into the process. Restorative justice programmes like mediation clearly offer victims input into the procedure and should therefore be an attractive option for them.

However, victims do not necessarily have to leave the criminal justice system in order to have some input into the procedure. Criminal justice procedure can be, and in several countries has been, modified to include victims. Examples include sentencing circles (where community members are invited to speak at the sentencing hearing), victim impact statements (where the victim can submit a written statement at the sentencing hearing), victim notification and victim consultation (simply informing and consulting with victims throughout the criminal justice process). These measures recognise the victim and his/her interest in the case without giving him/her decision-making power.

Victims do, however, have to resort to extrajudicial measures if they want to maintain decision control. It is not possible to give victims decision-making power in the traditional criminal justice system. Victims and offenders are likely to want to keep decision control only when they share common goals. In these cases, they are likely to be dissatisfied with the criminal justice system, which does not give them decision-making power. When the conflict is manageable, victims and offenders are likely to prefer restorative measures, like mediation, which place decision control in the hands of the parties.

However, procedural justice theory and research shows that decision control is relatively unimportant to victims (Wemmers 1996). Moreover, when victims and offenders do not share common goals, which will often be the case, they are likely to prefer third-party intervention. In these cases, the traditional criminal justice system, which places decision-making power in the hands of criminal justice authorities, should be satisfying to them.

If victims typically want input but do not want decision-making power, then they might prefer initiatives that incorporate restorative justice concepts within the traditional criminal justice system to extrajudicial measures like mediation. Third-party intervention is desirable to victims of crime, and they do not want to see the involvement of a neutral third party abolished or the responsibility of decision-making placed on their shoulders. The importance of third-party intervention shows that the restorative justice paradigm cannot, and should not, fully replace the traditional criminal justice model. While criminal justice reform is warranted, clearly the notion of a 'paradigm shift' goes too far.

The above findings suggest that restorative justice programmes are attractive to victims not because they offer victims control over the outcome, as Roach (1999) suggests, but because they allow the victim to have input in the procedure. The reluctance of criminal justice authorities to implement victim-friendly policies that include victims in the criminal justice process (see for example Wemmers 1996) makes extrajudicial measures an attractive option for victims. In these programmes victims can state their views and request restitution, an apology, or concrete services from the offender. While many countries have introduced victim-friendly policies and victims can often request restitution through the criminal justice process, in practice this rarely happens (Wemmers 1996; Groenhuijsen 1999). Hence, it may be easier for victims to be included in the process in extrajudicial programmes.

However, there are still several questions left unanswered. For example, how often do criminal cases involve correspondent outcomes? And would Thibaut and Walker's findings on procedural preferences be confirmed in a direct test among victims of crime? Clearly, further research is necessary in order to understand the wants and needs of victims of crime better.

Note

1.   Outcome-correspondence was created by varying the announced mode of payment for participation. Subjects in the correspondent condition were told that all members of the winning table in the second

competition would share alike in the winnings. Non-correspondence was created by telling subjects that only the person whose ranking was chosen would receive a bonus payment.

References

Christie N. (1977) 'Conflict as property.' *British Journal of Criminology* 17, 1, 1–15.

Erez E. and Tontodonato P. (1992) 'Victim participation in sentencing and satisfaction with justice.' *Justice Quarterly* 9, 3, 393–419.

Groenhuijsen M. (1999) 'Victims' rights in the criminal justice system: A call for more comprehensive implementation theory.' In J. van Dijk, R. van Kaam and J. Wemmers (eds.) *Caring for Victims.* Monsey: Criminal Justice Press.

Houlden P., LaTour S., Walker L. and Thibaut, J. (1978) 'Preferences for modes of dispute resolution as a function of process and decision control.' *Journal of Experimental Social Psychology* 14, 13–30.

Kelly D. and Erez E. (1997) 'Victim participation in the criminal justice system.' In R. Davis, A. Lurigio and W. Skogan (eds.) *Victims of Crime,* second edition. Thousand Oaks: Sage Publications.

Kilchling, M. (1995) *Offerinteressen und Strafverfolgung.* Freiburg: Max-Planck-Instituut fur Auslandisches und Internationales Strafrecht (dissertation).

Lind E.A. and Tyler T. (1988) *The Social Psychology of Procedural Justice.* New York: Plenum Press.

Pate K. (1990) 'Victim–offender reconciliation programs in Canada.' In B. Galaway and J. Hudson (eds.) *Criminal Justice, Restitution and Reconciliation.* Monsey NY: Criminal Justice Press, 135–145.

Roach K. (1999) *Due Process and Victims' Rights: The New Law and Politics of Criminal Justice.* Toronto: University of Toronto Press.

Shapland J., Willmore J. and Duff P. (1985) *Victims in the Criminal Justice System.* Aldershot: Gower.

Smale G.J.A. (1980) *Slachtoffers van ernstige vermogens- en geweldsmisdrijven: Deel II immateriele problematiek I.* Groningen: Kriminologisch Instituut.

Stuart B. (1996) 'Circle sentencing: turning swords into ploughshares.' In B. Galaway and J. Hudson (eds.) *Restorative Justice: International Perspectives.* Monsey NY: Criminal Justice Press, 193–206.

Thibaut J. and Walker L. (1975) *Procedural Justice: A Psychological Analysis.* Hillsdale NJ: John Wiley & Sons.

Tyler T.R. (1990) *Why People Obey the Law.* New Haven: Yale University Press.

Weitekamp E. (1999) 'The paradigm of restorative justice: Potentials, possibilities, and pitfalls.' In J. van Dijk, R. van Kaam and J. Wemmers (eds.) *Caring for Victims.* Monsey, NY: Criminal Justice Press, 115–126.

Wemmers J. and Van Hecke T. (1992) *Strafrechtelijke Dading.* Den Haag: Wetenschappelijk Onderzoek- en Documentatiecentrum. K23.

Wemmers J. (1994) *Evaluatie Terwee Slachtofferonderzoek Wet en Richtlijn Terwee: eindrapport.* The Hague: Wetenschappelijk Onderzoek en Documentatiecentrum, Ministerie van Justitie.

Wemmers J. (1996) *Victims in the Criminal Justice System.* Amsterdam/New York: Kugler.

4.

Family Group Conferencing

A Victim Perspective

Guy Masters

This chapter provides an overview of the development of family group conferences (FGCs), and reviews the current research evidence on whether and why victims of crime participate in conferences, and the impact that such participation has on those involved. Initially it provides an overview of the New Zealand youth justice system, which has made significant use of family group conferencing in youth justice since 1990. The emergence of a second 'conferencing' model in New South Wales, Australia, is also detailed, and the available research evidence for both models in relation to victims discussed. Where appropriate, comparisons will be made with the related research on victim–offender mediation. This chapter will predominantly focus on reviewing the quantitative evidence that has been gathered to date about how victims appear to experience conferencing. Any readers interested in reviewing case studies are recommended to see Moore and O'Connell (1994) and Roberts and Masters (1998), and Jackson (1998a), Maxwell and Morris (1996) or Morris, Maxwell and Robertson (1993) for qualitative comments from victims about their participation in FGCs.

The introduction of family group conferencing in New Zealand

FGCs were first developed in New Zealand following the Children, Young Person and their Families Act 1989. FGCs were intended to change fundamentally how professional agencies and courts made decisions about the children, young people and families that came to their attention on welfare grounds, or because offences had been committed by someone aged 14–17 (Justice 2000). Through FGCs the New Zealand authorities planned to enable young people and their families to play a far more significant role in decision-making that could radically affect their lives. This represents a belief that, given appropriate preparation, even those families considered the most dysfunctional are able to produce and implement innovative plans that address the concerns of professionals.

Within youth justice it was hoped that FGCs would enable the young person, their extended family, and any victims to produce collectively a plan of action that would be in the interests of both the young person and their victims. Youth justice FGCs are held at two points in the New Zealand youth justice system: either to enable a young person to be diverted from prosecution, or, when prosecution is considered appropriate, before a sentence is passed. In relation to court-ordered FGCs, only courts sentencing young people for murder or manslaughter are excluded from first having to consider a plan produced by an FGC.

FGCs are a central element of a system that was intended to divert the majority of young people from the formal justice system, and significantly reduce the use of custody for the minority that are not diverted. However, this should not be viewed as an experiment in non-intervention, but rather as an attempt to work with the majority of young people without formally bringing them into the youth justice system. Consequently, only around 10 per cent of young people who are apprehended are prosecuted. Of the remaining 90 per cent, one quarter are simply warned by the arresting officer, a little over one half (55%) are contacted by Police Youth Aid, which undertakes short stints of work with the young people and their families, and 10 per cent are referred for a diversionary FGC (Maxwell and Morris 1996). Almost all of the 10 per cent who are prosecuted will also experience an FGC. (See Table 4.1). The informal action taken by Police Youth Aid follows some investigation with the young person, their family, and victims, and may lead to apologies being facilitated, small amounts of community work being done, or small amounts of compensation being paid.

It is important to recognise that the views of crime victims are not ignored in cases that are not referred to an FGC. Indeed, if prosecution is not considered necessary, then one reason for considering a diversionary FGC in preference to more informal action is because the police assessment of the case has identified that the offence has had a significant impact upon the victims (Justice 2000).

Table 4.1 Outcomes for young people who have offended in New Zealand (aggregate date for 1991–1993 derived from Maxwell and Morris (1996, p.91)

Total cases 1991–1993	Warned	Youth Aid	Diversionary FGC	Prosecuted	Total
109,159	24%	58%	10%	9%	100%

Family group conferencing in practice

In this model referrals are passed to a co-ordinator to convene and facilitate the FGC. In New Zealand referrals are made to a 'youth justice co-ordinator' (an employee of the Department of Social Welfare) either by court or by the youth aid section of the Police. The coordinator, in cooperation with the young person and their family, will determine who should be invited to the FGC. In youth justice cases this is typically the young person, their immediate and extended family or carers, and others who are important to the young person or their family, and whom they wish to be present. One coordinator interviewed by the author reported asking a young person for a list of the people whom they would invite to an important celebration in their life, as an example of who should attend the FGC.

The victim or victims of the offences being considered by the FGC are also invited to attend, and they too are invited to bring 'supporters' with them. Initially, the legislation in New Zealand did not allow victims to be accompanied by supporters. However, in practice most co-ordinators did not interpret this rigidly, and the legislation was amended in 1994 to enable victim supporters to attend FGCs (Stewart 1996).

FGCs may also be attended by professionals who are already involved, or may become involved, with the family or the young person. These professionals are invited to the FGC as 'information givers', to inform the FGC about resources that are available and may be considered as potential elements of the plan. In New Zealand the youth aid police officer who investigated the case will also be present. Advocates can also attend FGCs in New Zealand. The advocate's role has developed into one that complements the spirit of the FGC; they focus on protecting the rights of young people under the legislation, rather than adopting an adversarial or mitigating role (Justice 2000).

In practice the FGC will be opened by the co-ordinator, who will then either introduce each of the participants, or ask them to introduce themselves. It is then usual for the attending police officer to detail the offences that the young person is accused of, and the defendant will be asked to accept or deny the charges. It is highly unlikely that the young person will deny all of the charges at this stage, as they would not have been eligible for an FGC if this were the case. However, it is possible that the young person will accept some of the charges. In this case the police must decide whether the FGC continues only considering the charges admitted by the young person, or whether the case will need to be referred to the court.

Once charges have been accepted, then the young person describes what occurred and their involvement in the offence. Co-ordinators ask follow-up questions of the young person to elicit their thoughts and feelings about the offence, at the time and since. The victim or victims are then invited to speak about their experience of the offence and any subsequent impact it has had on them. They are invited to ask questions of the young person and those assembled. This element of the conference often resembles victim–offender mediation (and the second conferencing model considered below), and could be described as the 'mediation' or 'offence resolution stage' of the FGC. Supporters of either victim(s) or offender(s) are entitled to join in with this discussion. This dialogue is often emotionally charged (see Roberts and Masters (1999) for case studies) and usually includes an apology to the victims, and possibly to others. It may also include some discussion of what the young person may be able to do to make amends to the victims.

Following this dialogue, other supporters are invited, if they have not already done so, to comment upon the situation leading to a wider discussion about the factors that may have precipitated the offending, and what action needs to be taken to prevent further offending. At this stage the 'information providers' may contribute to the FGC by discussing the young person's education, or what the particular concerns of social welfare agencies may be, etc.

This will then be followed by 'private planning time' for the young person and their supporters. It is this element of the FGC process that distinguishes this model from the second model that will be considered shortly. In the FGC model the young person, their family and supporters are left alone by everyone else (including the facilitator) to construct their plan, though they can invite other persons to join them or to clarify issues. There are no time limits upon this planning time.

Once a plan has been formed by the young person and their family, then the full FGC is reconvened to hear the plan. In New Zealand both the police and the victim have the power to veto the plan if they are not satisfied with it. What generally occurs is that elements of the plan are negotiated in this stage of the conference, including the matter of who (usually from among the offender's support group) will monitor that it is being implemented. The private family planning time and the final stage of the conference can be considered as the 'action planning' part of the conference.

In summary, then, youth justice FGCs can be considered as consisting of

(1)   introductions and the young person accepting the charges

(2)   an offence resolution or mediation stage

(3)   an information and action planning stage (including private planning time), followed by the close of the conference.

Some commentators consider that the private planning time in this model indicates that the principle aim of the youth justice FGC model is family empowerment. The victims and professionals present are invited to attend in order to provide information for the young person and the family to consider in making their plan (Jackson 1998b). Some commentators have expressed concern that this provision of private time may leave victims feeling excluded or offended, and that they may interpret this as giving the offender and their family priority over the victim (Wright 1996). Observations by the author in New Zealand suggest that in at least some cases the Youth Aid officer and the co-ordinator use the private time to consult with victim(s) about their experience of the FGC so far, and to check whether there are any issues that they felt unable to voice in the first part of the conference, and what level of reparation they expect in the plan. This would suggest that the private time can offer a useful opportunity for victims to express to the co-ordinator any concerns that they may have, also in privacy. However, whether victims do regularly feel marginalised through private planning time is a question for further research.

FGCs in England and Wales

Following their widespread introduction in New Zealand in 1990, other countries have been quick to experiment with FGCs (see Hudson *et al.* 1996). In England and Wales, a number of FGC projects were launched in the early 1990s in child welfare, and considered successful (Marsh and Crow 1998). The use of FGCs in youth justice in England and Wales has taken longer to develop, with only several small pilot projects (for example the Kent Intensive Support and Supervision Programme, the Hampton Trust FGC project in Hampshire, and the Sunderland Focused Caution Scheme) developing until very recently. However, through the Youth Justice Board for England and Wales, development funds are available for 'restorative justice schemes', and the number and scope of FGC projects has quickly expanded.

Development of the Wagga conferencing model

The second model of conferencing also currently in widespread use was developed by Terry O'Connell, while Senior Sergeant with the New South Wales Police (Australia), and based in Wagga Wagga. This model has now been given a variety of different names in different jurisdictions around the world, for example, 'restorative conferencing', 'diversionary conferencing', 'community conferencing', and also (unhelpfully) 'family group conferencing'. For the purpose of this chapter, this model will be referred to as 'restorative conferencing', the title by which it is best known in the United Kingdom.

This model was first developed as part of an 'Effective Cautioning Project' in 1991 (Moore and O'Connell 1994). It was hoped to divert more young people away from formal processing by the court and to provide a high level of satisfaction to victims. Drawing on the experience of family group conferencing in New Zealand, the police in Wagga Wagga created a project whereby young people would be diverted from court into conferences that would be facilitated by a police officer. It was intended that these conferences would seek to explore the full extent of the harm caused by an offence, or several offence(s). These conferences sought to bring together the young person, or persons, responsible for the offence, with their family and other supporters, as well as the victims and any supporters that the victims wished to bring.

Restorative conferences focus on exploring, in detail, the thoughts and feelings of all of those present at the conference, both at the time of the offence, and since the offence. Restorative conferences are structured so that the co-ordinator asks similar questions to each of the participants in a certain order.

Following introductions, the young person/people describe what they did, and what they thought and felt about it at the time of the offence. They are then asked to describe who they think has been affected and in what way.

The primary victims of the offence (i.e. those against whom the offence was directly committed) will be asked about the offence from their perspective, how they felt at the time and subsequently. The offenders may be asked to respond at this stage, or the co-ordinator may ask any supporters of the victims to describe how the offence affected them, and/or their perceptions of its impact upon the primary victim(s).

Following this the offender's family and supporters are asked to comment on the effect of the offence upon them, and their thoughts and feelings about the offence and the young offender. The young person is then asked to respond to all of this, and apologies to all involved are reported as being very forthcoming. The literature on this model of conferencing stresses that the co-ordinators also seek to have supporters of the offender identify the strengths and positive aspects of the offender's character so that the offender does not experience the conference as stigmatising (Braithwaite and Mugford 1994). Once all participants have been able to fully discuss the impact of the offence(s) upon them, the conference will consider whether anything needs to be done to make up for the offence, such as written apologies, financial compensation, or community service work as reparation. There is generally no professional information-giving stage or private planning time in this model. At the end of the conference, refreshments are sometimes provided so that communication can continue beyond the formal end of conference.

This model of conferencing has been explicitly linked with John Braithwaite's (1989) theory of 'reintegrative shaming'. The links between reintegrative shaming, other shame theory, conferencing and restorative justice in general are explored by Braithwaite and Mugford (1994), Masters (1998), and Moore and Forsyth (1995).

Restorative Conferencing in England and Wales

In England and Wales, Thames Valley Police have actively championed the development of restorative conferencing as an alternative to the traditional cautioning process, which they saw as a passive process that also ignored the views and needs of any victims. Widespread use of this model throughout

England and Wales seems likely, following the training of 700 police officers and Youth Offending Team staff as conference facilitators in 2000.

What is the role of the victim in these forums?

Before considering the role of victims in these forums, and how beneficial victims of crime consider these forums to be, it is important to note the complexity of this issue. Both models of conferencing, while structured to a certain extent, are designed to elicit open discussion among participants of the issues that are important to them. Participants are able to ask each other about their experiences and their current circumstances.

One result of this discussion is that the labels 'offender' and 'victim', are difficult to maintain (also a common occurrence in victim–offender mediation (see Marshall and Merry 1990)). For instance, information revealed about a young person attending a conference as 'the offender' may indicate that they have experienced degrees of victimisation in their lives, either from individuals or from various systems. To take another example, it is often recognised that the impact of the offence upon the offender's family identifies them as additional victims of the offence. The restorative conferencing model was explicitly designed to develop this dimension.

This complexity has been explored in detail by Young (2000), who concludes that the use of labels such as 'victim' and 'offender' is not particularly helpful. At the very least, Young recommends, we should adopt approaches that recognise the possibility of multiple victimisation when considering restorative approaches. (While agreeing entirely with Young, this chapter will consider 'the direct victim' to be the person against whom the offence was primarily committed).

The role of the victim in the conferencing models

The role of, and potential benefits for, victims in either conferencing model are almost the same as for victims who participate in victim–offender mediation. In summary, victims have the opportunity to meet the offender, explain how they were affected by the offence and ask questions relating to why and how the offence was committed. It is now well established that many victims appreciate such opportunities (Marshall and Merry 1990; Umbreit 1994). Victims are likely to receive explanations and apologies. All available research suggests that both are highly valued by victims of crime (for example, see Hayes *et al.* (1998); Marshall and Merry (1990); Morris *et al.* (1993); Strang *et al.* (1999); Umbreit 1994; Wright (1996)). Victims can also request financial or material compensation (direct reparation), and/or make suggestions about community work that can be undertaken as (indirect) reparation for the offence. In the FGC model, victims can also make suggestions about, and comment upon, activities included in the plan with the intention of preventing further offending.

The main findings on research with victims who have experienced FGCs or restorative conferences

Do victims wish to attend FGCs?

The first point to consider is whether victims actually wish to attend such meetings with offenders. Unlike victim–offender mediation, an FGC can go ahead without any direct victims of the offence being present. Research conducted by Maxwell and Morris (1993) evaluating the New Zealand experience of FGCs is of significant interest. Maxwell and Morris (1993) found that victims only attended FGCs in 51 per cent of cases in which there was an identifiable victim. Follow-up with those victims who did not attend FGCs is revealing: only 6 per cent of victims did not attend because they did not wish to meet the offender. The majority of victims did not attend the FGC because of 'poor practice', i.e. they were either not invited at all, invited at very short notice, or were invited to an FGC held at a time inconvenient for them. Interestingly, Morris *et al.* (1993) note that the majority of victims who did not attend FGCs were those involved in the more minor offences (only 12 per cent of conferences on minor offences had victims present)[1]. After visiting two different areas in New Zealand, Justice (2000) reports that victim attendance and satisfaction both appeared to vary substantially between the two areas.

This finding is backed up by the experience of other jurisdictions that almost certainly had greater human resources available to convene conferences, and sought to do so at the convenience of victims. For example, evaluation of 'youth justice conferencing' introduced in New South Wales in 1998 (based on the family group conferencing model) reports a 73 per cent victim participation rate (Trimboli 2000). Commenting on the initial introduction of family group conferencing in South Australia, Wundersitz and Hetzel (1996, p.123) report that 'preliminary evidence suggests that 75–80% of those conferences involving a victim-based crime have at least one victim present'. This supports the earlier claims of the police-led conferencing model developed in Wagga Wagga, where a deliberate effort was made to make victims feel important, and which, it is claimed, led to high levels of victim involvement (Moore and O'Connell 1994). Unfortunately, the evaluation of this project (Moore and Forsyth 1995) does not provide any quantitative evidence to substantiate these claims. However, the experience of 'community conferencing' in Queensland, which operates at a similar point to the Wagga scheme (but uses independent co-ordinators) does provide supportive statistics. The evaluators (Hayes *et al.* 1998) report that of 143 referrals, 111 conferences (77%) took place with victims in attendance. Similarly, the experience of the Reintegrative Shaming Experiment (RISE) in Canberra, Australian Capital Territory, which does use police co-ordinators, is that victims attended 73 per cent of conferences held for offences against personal property, and 90 per cent of conferences held for violent incidents (Strang *et al.* 1999).

FGCs in England and Wales

To date there is limited data available about whether victims attend FGCs in England and Wales. The pilot FGC project run by the Hampton Trust convened 12 FGCs between April 1997 and March 1998 (out of 16 referrals). Victims attended seven of these FGCs. (Although percentages must be used with caution in view of the low number of cases, for the sake of comparison this represents a participation rate of 58%.) However, the evaluation notes that,

> Of victims not attending, it was generally indirect victims prevented by lack of support or interest from employers (4), with some employees expected to attend in personal time and 1 personal victim unable to attend due to an unavoidable last minute clash of appointments. No general reluctance to attend was identified for either direct or indirect victims, although some shops seemed less inclined to send representative as time progressed. (Jackson 1998a, p.34).

This supports the findings in New Zealand, where 'Almost all the victims we interviewed welcomed this opportunity [to attend an FGC] and said that either they attended or would have been pleased to attend if that had been possible' (Morris *et al.* 1993, p.309).

The conclusion is that victims will attend a conference if they are invited to one that is held at a time suitable and convenient for them. It is important to note that the schemes that are successful in involving victims are those that have the resources to invest a significant amount of time undertaking pre-conference preparation work with all of the parties invited to the conference. Jackson (1998a) reports that FGC co-ordinators in Hampshire spent an average of 23 hours preparing participants, and Hayes *et al.* (1998, p.22) comment on the importance of the intake process 'to ensure that victims were protected and that young people gain maximum benefit'. Justice (2000) reports that in areas of New Zealand where the local Youth Justice Co-ordinators have adequate time to prepare participants for FGCs, local victim attendance is very high.

Comparison with victim–offender mediation

Mark Umbreit (1995) reports that of 4,445 referrals made to four Canadian victim–offender mediation projects between 1991 and 1993, direct mediation took place in 1,736 cases (39%). Similarly, of 3,142 referrals made to four victim–offender mediation projects in the USA, 1131 (36%) led to direct mediation. Umbreit and Roberts (1996) report that 35 per cent of 272 referrals to one victim–offender mediation project in England (Coventry) resulted in either indirect or direct mediation, while 49 per cent of 535 referrals to another (Leeds) led to mediation. Victim attendance at conferences appears, then, to be quite substantially higher than for victim–offender mediation projects. While this has yet to be the subject of detailed research, one possible reason may be the two quite different opportunities that each presents for victims. Victims may opt to attend an event that they know is going to go ahead with or without them (i.e. an FGC), so as to ensure that their views are adequately represented (for example see Morris *et al.* (1993) and below). Mediation, however, will only take place if the victim accepts an offer to participate. One concern in relation to this stems from research investigating victim participation rates in services provided by Victim Support in the UK (Wilkinson and Maguire 1990). This research identified those victims most likely to benefit from involvement with Victim Support as those most likely to decline their services. It is possible that the same applies to victims invited to participate in mediation, and this deserves research attention.

How do victims experience FGCs and restorative conferences?

Before considering the actual experiences of victims in FGCs it is important to acknowledge that, like victim–offender mediation, FGCs and restorative conferences are only likely to meet a limited range of needs for victims. For example, it is unlikely that any significant financial losses could ever be fully compensated for by a conference arrangement, or that it could ever completely make up for significant emotional harm and anger incurred by an offence. Such limitations have been recognised in practice. Most implementation guides strongly recommend pre-conference preparation which explores realistic outcomes of the FGC, so that decisions to participate are based on realistic assessments of the potential risks and benefits for participants (for example, see Levine *et al.* (undated), Youth Justice Board/Crime Concern 2000).

Morris *et al.* (1993, p.309) state that victims reported attending FGCs in New Zealand for a number of reasons. First, because they perceived attendance to be in their interests: they requested reparation, confronted the offender, related their feelings about what has happened, and 'ensured that things were done properly'. Second, because they wanted to help or support the young person; and third, a small number attended because they believed that victims should attend such meetings in principle, or from curiosity.

Sixty per cent of victims who attended FGCs found them 'helpful, positive, and rewarding' (Morris *et al.* 1993, p.11), reporting that they came to have a better understanding of why the offence happened, and/or that this was a cathartic experience enabling them to release negative feelings. Victims also reported benefiting from the opportunity to be involved in determining appropriate outcomes, and from being able to meet and find out more about the offender and their family.

However, 25 per cent of victims felt worse following the FGC. The principle reasons for this were that they remembered negative feelings relating to the offence; thought that the FGC outcomes were inadequate; perceived a lack of remorse on the part of the offender; or they felt worse due to the extent of the offending. In relation to FGC plans, 62 per cent of victims agreed with the decisions that were made at the FGC, while 35 per cent would have liked more penalties of reparation, and 8 per cent would have liked to see more welfare for the young person featuring in the plan. While 25 per cent is a disappointing figure, the authors consider that much of this victim dissatisfaction may stem from 'the lack of adequate briefing for victims about their role in FGCs and what they might realistically expect'. (Morris *et al.* 1993, p.315) and the abilities of co-ordinators 'without much training …to manage such emotional and, by their nature, unpredictable meetings' (Morris *et al.* 1993, p.314).

That this is so *may* be supported by the findings from evaluations of other projects outside New Zealand. For example, evaluation of youth justice conferencing in New South Wales found overall levels of participation and victim satisfaction to be very high. Trimboli (2000) found that 94 per cent of victims felt that they had been treated fairly in the conference and that their views had been taken into account. Eighty-nine per cent reported being satisfied with the plan, and that the outcome was fair to them. Of note is that when asked for the best features of how their conferences were run, 89 per cent of victims (233) had something positive to say, while only 2 per cent (5) of victims reported that there were 'no good features'.

Slightly fewer victims (77%) considered the 'conference took adequate account of the effects of the offence' on them. Victims were also asked about the best and worst features of the conference plans. Twenty-eight per cent chose not to answer the question, 37 per cent reported that there were no negative features, and 36 per cent said that there were some negative features. Of this latter group of 94 victims, 22 (8% of all victims) thought the plan contained 'insufficient/untimely compensation for damage', 20 (8%) considered that the plan was 'lenient on the offender', and 14 (5%) that the plan had not been completed (Trimboli 2000, p.48). Finally, 79 per cent of all victims reported that they were 'satisfied with the way [their] case had been handled by the justice system'.

Hayes *et al.* (1998) report on the views of victims who have experienced community conferencing in Queensland (the restorative conferencing model). This evaluation found that 98 per cent of victims (88) thought that the conference was fair, and 97 per cent were satisfied with the agreements that were made. A follow-up survey two to four months after the initial survey found that 94 per cent of victims still thought that the conference had been fair, and that 93 per cent were still satisfied with the agreement that had been made. Eighty-seven per cent of victims reported that the conference had helped them cope with the offence. All victims who had experienced conferences would recommend them to other victims, and agreed that conferences were 'a good way of dealing with young people who have committed offences'. However, 15 per cent of victims reported that if they 'had their time over' they would rather have gone to court. While this is not a discouraging response, it does suggest a slight inconsistency with the satisfaction ratings.

A second evaluation of the restorative conferencing model is that of RISE in Canberra (Strang *et al.* 1999).The RISE evaluation is particularly interesting as it compares the experiences of victims who participated in conferences held for personal property offences[2] with those held for violent offences[3]. Table 4.2 summarises these findings, which support those from New Zealand – that it is the victims of more serious offences that are more likely to attend, but also more likely to be dissatisfied (Morris *et al.* 1993). However, as a significant minority of violent cases were also 'conferenced' in both Queensland[4] and New South Wales[5] with good results, it remains a question for further research whether conferences on violent offences are more likely to leave victims dissatisfied, or whether this reflects a need for different practice.

Table 4.2 Victim experiences of RISE conferences		
Item	Personal property	Violence
Attended the conference	73%	90%
Felt that the conference was fair to me	97%	77%
Felt too intimidated to speak during the conference	3%	15%
Had an opportunity to express my views in the conference	91%	84%
Conference took account of what I said in reaching a decision	91%	69%
Conference took account of the effects the offence had on me	85%	65%
Felt pushed into things I did not agree with	3%	13%
Felt I was treated with respect at the conference	91%	69%
The [conference] made me feel angry	16%	23%
Feel bitter about the way I was treated	10%	23%
Satisfied with the outcome after conference	80%	56%
Satisfied with way case was dealt with	60%	68%

The RISE evaluation (Strang *et al.* 1999) also measured the 'restorative' impact of conferences upon victims, and again some interesting differences emerged. What is clear from Table 4.3 is that while there are emotional benefits for victims of both personal property and violence offences, it is the latter group who appear to have more to gain (as well as possibly more to lose).

Table 4.3 Impact of RISE conference for victims		
Item	Personal property	Violence
Felt angry with offender before [the conference]	60%	69%
Felt angry with offender after [the conference]	23%	31%
Felt sympathetic to the offender before [the conference]	23%	12%
Felt sympathetic to the offender before [the conference]	60%	36%
Felt afraid of offender before [the conference]	6%	31%
Felt afraid of offender after the [conference]	3%	12%
Conference made me feel that I could put the whole thing behind me	66%	62%
Conference made me feel more emotionally settled	38%	44%
Felt that my sense of security has been restored	65%	80%
Anticipate offender will revictimise me	13%	4%

The statistics in Table 4.3 partially illustrate the potential 'restorative' (Wright 1996) or 'transformative' (Moore and Forsyth 1995) impact of conferencing for victims. As with victim–offender mediation (Marshall and Merry 1990; Umbreit 1994), it is apparent that participation in conferences *can* lead to what would appear to be a significant level of 'healing', 'closure' or 'recovery'. To date, there has been no systematic attempt to quantify how common such occurrences are for victims, though the statistics reported here from RISE suggest that they are not infrequent. For example, the proportion of victims who still feel angered by the offence falls significantly, as does fear of further victimisation, and a significant minority of victims report feeling 'more emotionally settled' after the conference. Strang and Sherman (1997, p.3) report the following anecdotal comment which gives some life to these statistics:

> I had this enormous amount of anger that I wanted to shout out, but I felt very defensive. I was so angry that I was sitting there literally shaking. Then as the conference got under way I was able to say all the things I'd been thinking about for all those weeks and explain how angry I was...to put him in the picture of how it affected us made me feel so much better...I felt a great sense of relief of getting it off my chest.

There is also evidence from Queensland that these benefits are not a minority occurrence. Hayes *et al.* (1998, p.32) report that 82 per cent of victims considered that the conference helped them deal with the consequences of the offence. Morris *et al.* (1993, p.316) comment on New Zealand that

> reconciliation...did clearly occur on occasions. At one FGC we observed, after tearful apologies had been made by both the youth and his family, there seemed to be a reluctance amongst the parties to leave the meeting. There were handshakes and embraces all round and finally a suggestion by one of the victims that the offender and his family join him for a meal at a later date.

While the long term sustainability of these benefits is still to be established, it seems that for many victims the potential benefits of participation in conferencing are substantial.

Conclusion

The evidence, primarily from New Zealand and Australia, suggests that if conferences are held at a convenient time, a majority of victims are interested in attending either family group or restorative conferences, particularly victims of more serious offences. The similar results obtained by the

Hampton Trust FGC project stand in stark contrast to the experience of recent attempts to involve victims in reparation elements of the 1998 Crime & Disorder Act in England and Wales (see Dignan 2000), and particularly to involve victims in mediation.

The research evaluation figures illustrate that a majority of victims do report that they benefit from this experience. It appears that victims of serious and violent offences have the most to gain from participation.

It also clear that a small minority of victims have been both disappointed and traumatised by their conference experience (Morris *et al.*1993). While a minority of victims reported feeling worse following participation in either model of conferences, it seems that this was at least partially due to poor preparation which left victims with unrealistic expectations for their confer-ence. This could almost certainly be minimised through high quality prepa-ratory work which assesses whether their expectations are likely to be met or not.

Notwithstanding the overall generally positive findings about the experi-ence of victims in conferences, as other commentators have noted (Morris *et al.* 1993), no form of conferencing or mediation should ever be the sole process for providing support and assistance to victims. Victims of crime often have multiple needs that can only be addressed through wider social policy. No matter what level of resources is invested to develop family group conferencing, restorative conferencing, or victim–offender mediation, the introduction of a comprehensive system for addressing all the needs of all crime victims is required before any jurisdiction can claim to have a fully re-storative justice system.

Notes

1. Statistics derived from Maxwell and Morris (1996, p.93) who detail that 32 per cent of all diversionary and court ordered FGCs are held for burglary, 22 per cent for theft or fraud, 18 per cent for assault, robbery or sexual offences, 16 per cent for car conversion, 4 per cent for drugs or anti-social behaviour, 2 per cent for property damage, and 8 per cent for other offences.

2. The personal property offence category consisted of generic theft 33 per cent, shop theft 26 per cent, vandalism/criminal damage 20 per cent, burglary 13 per cent, auto theft 5 per cent, and receive/possess stolen goods 3 per cent. The violent offences category consisted of common assault 52 per cent,

actual/grievous bodily harm 18 per cent, arson 15 per cent, fighting 6 per cent, robbery 6 per cent, and other violence 3 per cent.

3. Offenders up to the age of 30 were included in the violence category.

4. Fifty-one per cent of conferences in Queensland were held for either theft or burglary, 21 per cent for damage to property, 16 per cent for assault, 3 per cent for drug offences, 2 per cent for robbery, 2 per cent for driving and traffic offences, and 1 per cent for fraud, and 5 per cent for other offences (see Hayes *et al.* 1998, p.37).

5. Thirty per cent of conferences in New South Wales were held for theft related offences, 19 per cent for burglary, 16 per cent for assault, 12 per cent for criminal damage, 7 per cent for public order offences, 7 per cent for deception, 3 per cent for robbery, and 5 per cent for other offences (see Trimboli 2000, p.29).

References

Braithwaite J. (1989) *Crime, Shame and Reintegration.* Cambridge: Cambridge University Press.

Braithwaite J. and Mugford S. (1994) 'Conditions of successful reintegration ceremonies: Dealing with juvenile offenders.' *British Journal of Criminology* 34, 2, 139–171.

Dignan J. (2000) *Youth Justice Pilots Evaluation: Interim Report on Reparative Work and Youth Offending Teams.* London: Home Office.

Hayes H., Prenzler T. and Wortley R. (1998) *Making Amends: Final Evaluation of the Queensland Community Conferencing Pilot.* Queensland: Griffith University.

Hudson J., Morris A., Maxwell G. and Galaway B. (1996) *Family Group Conferences: Perspectives on Policy and Practice.* New York: Willow Tree Press.

Jackson S. (1998a) *Family Justice? An Evaluation of the Hampshire Youth Justice Family Group Conferencing Project.* Southampton: University of Southampton.

Jackson S. (1998b) 'Family group conferencing in youth justice: The issues for implementation in England and Wales.' *Howard Journal of Criminal Justice* 37, 1, 34–51.

Justice (2000) *Restoring Youth Justice.* London: JUSTICE.

Levine M., Eagle A., Tuiavi'i S. and Roseveare C. (undated) *Creative Youth Justice Practice.* Wellington: Social Policy Agency and Children, Young Persons and their Families Service.

Marsh P. and Crow G. (1998) *Family Group Conferences in Child Welfare.* London: Blackwell.

Marshall T. and Merry S. (1990) *Crime and Accountability. Victim–Offender Mediation in Practice.* London: HMSO.

Masters G. (1998) 'The importance of shame to restorative justice.' In L. Walgrave (ed.) *Restorative Justice for Juveniles: Potentialities, Risks and Problems for Research.* Leuven: Leuven University Press.

Maxwell, G. and Morris, A. (1993) *Family Victims and Culture: Youth Justice in New Zealand* Wellington: Social Policy Agency and Institute of Criminology, Victoria University.

Maxwell G. and Morris A. (1996) 'Research on family group conferences with young offenders in New Zealand.' In J. Hudson, A. Morris, G. Maxwell and B. Galaway (eds.) *Family Group Conferences: Perspectives on Policy and Practice.* New York: Willow Tree Press.

Moore D. and Forsyth L. (1995) *A New Approach to Juvenile Justice: An Evaluation of Family Conferencing in Wagga Wagga.* New South Wales: Charles Sturt University: Centre for Rural Social Research.

Moore D. and O'Connell T. (1994) 'Family conferencing in Wagga Wagga: A communitarian model of justice.' In C. Alder and J. Wundersitz (eds.) *Family Conferencing and Juvenile Justice: The Way Forward or Misplaced Optimism?* Canberra: Australian Institute of Criminology.

Morris A., Maxwell G. and Robertson J. (1993) 'Giving victims a voice: A New Zealand experiment.' *Howard Journal of Criminal Justice* 32, 4, 304–321.

Roberts A. and Masters G. (1999) *Group Conferencing: Restorative Justice in Action.* Minnesota: University of Minnesota: Center for Restorative Justice and Mediation.

Stewart T. (1996) 'Family group conferences with young offenders in New Zealand.' In J. Hudson, A. Morris, G. Maxwell and B. Galaway (eds.) *Family Group Conferences: Perspectives on Policy and Practice.* New York: Willow Tree Press.

Strang H. and Sherman L. (1997) *RISE Working Papers: Paper No. 2. The Victim's Perspective.* Canberra: Australian National University.

Strang H., Barnes G., Braithwaite J. and Sherman L. (1999) *Experiments In Restorative Policing: A Progress Report on the Canberra Reintegrative Shaming Experiments (RISE).* Canberra: Australian National University.

Trimboli L. (2000) *An Evaluation of the NSW Youth Justice Conferencing Scheme.* New South Wales: Bureau of Crime Statistics and Research.

Umbreit M. (1994) *Victim Meets Offender.* New York: Willow Tree Press.

Umbreit M. (1995) *Mediation of Criminal Conflict in England: An Assessment of Programs in Four Canadian Provinces.* Minnesota: Centre for Restorative Justice and Mediation.

Umbreit M. and Roberts A. (1996) *Mediation of Criminal Conflict in England: An Assessment of Services in Coventry and Leeds.* Minnesota: Centre for Restorative Justice and Mediation.

Wilkinson C. and Maguire M. (1990) *Contacting Victims: Victim Support and the Relative Merits of Letters, Telephone Calls and Visits.* London: Home Office.

Wright M. (1996) *Justice for Victims and Offenders.* 2nd edition. Winchester: Waterside Press.

Wundersitz J. and Hetzel S. (1996) 'Family conferencing for young offenders: The South Australian experience.' In J. Hudson, A. Morris, G. Maxwell and B. Galaway (eds.) *Family Group Conferences: Perspectives on Policy and Practice.* New York: Willow Tree Press.

Young R. (2000) 'Integrating a multi-victim perspective into criminal justice through restorative justice conferences.' In A. Crawford and J. Goodey (eds.) *Integrating a Victim Perspective into Criminal Justice.* Aldershot: Ashgate.

Youth Justice Board for England and Wales/Crime Concern (2000) *Guidance on Developing Restorative Practice with Young Offenders and Victims of Crime.* London: Youth Justice Board for England and Wales.

5.

Reparation Orders

Jim Dignan

Introduction

'Reparation' is not synonymous with 'restorative justice', though the two concepts are often associated with one another. Reparation means making amends, and in a criminal justice context refers to action that is undertaken by an offender to repair the damage that may have been caused by an offence. Reparation can be made in various ways, for example by apologising; by physically restoring, replacing or repairing damaged property; by providing financial compensation or performing some service for or on behalf of a victim; or by seeking to address the psychological or emotional suffering that may have been caused by an offence. The latter may involve an offender acknowledging responsibility, providing information, offering reassurance or making commitments about future behaviour. The term 'reparation' can refer both to the process that is involved in making amends, for example the act of apologising to the victim in person, and also to the outcome, though it may not always be possible to differentiate between the two. Reparation can be made directly to the victim or indirectly, as when an offender makes amends by doing something that will benefit some other person, organisation or the community at large.

Reparation often plays an integral part in restorative justice processes, such as victim offender mediation, family group or community conferencing and circle sentencing.[1] Although there are important differences between them, such processes share the following four key attributes that are associated with a restorative justice approach (Dignan and Lowey 2000, p.4ff):

(1) in resolving an offence they first seek to address the interests of *both* the victim and the offender

(2) they encourage *participation* on the part of both parties, in determining an appropriate response

(3) they favour a forward-looking, *problem-solving approach*

(4) they favour voluntary participation and *non-coercive* procedures and outcomes.

However, reparation can also feature in the standard repertoire of more overtly punitive measures within a conventional, court-based, retributive criminal justice system. Until recently, the only form of reparation that was available within the mainstream English and Welsh criminal justice system consisted of the compensation order (see Cavadino and Dignan 1997 Chapter 8; 2001 Chapter 5). However, the concept of reparation featured prominently in the programme of youth justice reforms that was introduced under the Crime and Disorder Act 1998 and Youth Justice and Criminal Evidence Act 1999. While the reform programme as a whole incorporated some important elements of a restorative justice approach, the context in which they operate is still shaped largely by the traditional criminal justice process (Dignan 1999; Morris and Gelsthorpe 2000; Williams 2000). The result has been aptly described (Victim Support 1999) as a new and radical, hybrid form of justice that is neither purely restorative nor purely retributive, but incorporates elements of both approaches.

This chapter focuses specifically on the reparation order, which was introduced by the Crime and Disorder Act. (The Act also provided for reparative interventions to be undertaken in connection with final warnings and action plan orders, and as an additional condition in conjunction with supervision orders.[2]) The 1998 youth justice reforms, including the reparation order, were piloted in four different parts of the country[3] for a period of 18 months prior to national implementation of the entire reform programme in June 2000. During that period several aspects of the reform programme, including the reparation order, were independently evaluated. The main aim of this chapter is to summarise the principal findings of that evaluation insofar as it relates to the reparation order. But first it will be necessary to briefly outline the key features of the reparation order itself, the way it was evaluated and also the main institutional and operational contexts in which it was implemented and developed within the four pilot areas.

Reparation orders

The reparation order has two principal aims. The first is to help prevent further offending by bringing home to young offenders the consequences of their behaviour. The second is to require them to make amends for what they have done, either to their victim(s) – if the latter consent to this – or to the wider community, as appropriate. If the needs of victims are to be met in this way, it is clearly important for them to be routinely consulted before the content of a reparation order is finally determined.

Various kinds of reparation are possible under the Crime and Disorder Act[4], including meeting with the victim, which provides an opportunity to discuss the offence and its effects, and affords an opportunity for a direct apology to be made. Alternatively, reparation could involve the offender writing a letter of apology or undertaking some form of practical activity that benefits the victim(s) or the community at large. Financial reparation is not allowed, however, unless separately ordered by the court in the form of a compensation order.

The reparation order is variable in length (up to a maximum of 24 hours), though it has to be proportionate to the seriousness of the offence, and has to be completed within three months. It appears to be envisaged as an appropriate 'entry level' penalty for less serious offenders and others for whom a conditional discharge might have been considered appropriate in the past, though it is not restricted to such offenders. However, courts are obliged to give reasons for not imposing a reparation order in cases where they have the power to do so.

Reparation order evaluation

The youth justice reforms that were piloted under the Crime and Disorder Act were independently evaluated by a team of researchers from the Universities of Sheffield, Hull and Swansea. The evaluation was funded by the Home Office and examined the establishment and development of the pilot Youth Offending Teams.[5] It also examined the delivery of each of the main new youth justice interventions, focusing on process, outputs and outcomes. An additional report (Dignan 2000) focusing specifically on the 'process' lessons associated with the reparative work of the YOTs was also made available to the pilots during the evaluation.

Four main sets of data sources in respect of each of the pilot sites were drawn upon for the reparation order evaluation. They included case file records relating to 602 reparation orders, interview data relating to those who participated in a limited number of case studies,[6] interviews with a small sample of magistrates and court executives, and sentencing data provided by the Home Office Crime and Criminal Justice Unit.

Implementational issues relating specifically to the pilot YOTS

The decision to pilot and evaluate the 1998 youth justice reforms before implementing the policy nationally was innovative. Pilot areas were selected by the Home Office and represented a variety of different geographical locations and local government structures (Holdaway *et al.* 2001, p.47). They included a single and an overlapping court jurisdiction, a whole constabulary as well as several selected police divisions, and combinations of different local authority areas. In terms of populations, the latter ranged in size from 200,000 to 1.5 million.

The pilots faced an extremely tight timetable to establish not only the novel institutional and structural arrangements required by a fully functioning Youth Offending Team (see below), but also the protocols, procedures and programmes that are needed to deliver a range of new orders to the courts. Consequently, although the pilot areas provided invaluable lessons for other authorities, they were unable to avail themselves of the same thorough planning mechanisms that were envisaged in the 1998 Act. The latter included full youth justice plans based on an evidence-led assessment of local needs and best practice. Moreover, the need to prioritise the delivery of new services with a minimum of guidance from central government greatly constrained the time available for team-building and professional development, and also for training YOT team members and consulting with other relevant agencies.

It is important to bear these very real implementational constraints in mind when considering the results of the pilot reparation order evaluation, since the experience in non-pilot areas is likely to be very different in many respects. For example, important lessons from the YOT pilots and elsewhere have been incorporated in new national standards for youth justice and other more specific guidance published by the Youth Justice Board (2000)[7]. Where problems are identified in the national evaluation, therefore, it should not automatically be assumed that they are necessarily 'systemic', though some difficulties undoubtedly do fall into this category, as we shall see.

Institutional and operational contexts for delivering reparation orders

The responsibility for delivering reparation orders rests with the multi-agency youth offending teams[8] that were themselves established by the Crime and Disorder Act 1998. However, the Act provided considerable discretion in determining how to discharge this responsibility, and the pilots adopted a number of different arrangements. Three distinct models for delivering reparative interventions in particular can be identified within the pilot YOTs (Holdaway *et al.* 2001, p.82), and we have referred to these as the 'in-house', 'out-sourced' and 'mixed economy' models.

Within the 'in-house' model, the YOT itself retains sole responsibility for assessing offenders, consulting with victims and delivering all reparative interventions, using specially recruited and trained staff. The big advantage for the pilot which adopted this model was that it allowed for an early and relatively trouble-free implementation of the new measures, based on an effective assessment procedure and good communications with the rest of the YOT. However, very few criminal justice practitioners have the training and skills needed for this kind of work and, until this position changes, the potential for this model is likely to remain limited. Another drawback is that it affords relatively limited scope for community involvement in the delivery of reparative interventions, compared with the next model in particular.

Several of the pilots adopted an 'out-sourced' model whereby the responsibility for delivering certain aspects of the reparation (and other) orders is 'contracted out' to non-statutory, 'not-for-profit' organisations. The precise arrangements varied but, typically, responsibility for contacting victims and assessing the suitability of offenders was retained within the YOT, which then referred cases to a local service provider to 'deliver' the reparative intervention. Depending on the nature of the order this might involve setting up an appropriate community-based reparative task or activity, and supervising an offender, or alternatively facilitating a mediation meeting, negotiating the performance of a direct reparative task for the victim, or arranging some form of victim awareness activity.

The time taken to draw up contract specifications and let the contracts caused some short-term difficulties for two pilot areas in particular, and delayed the availability of a full range of reparative interventions. However, there was also evidence that an 'out-sourced' model could work well once these initial teething problems are resolved. The biggest long-term challenge is for the service provider to develop constructive relationships with both YOT and court. Not all the pilot areas that adopted this model rose to the challenge, but some were successful and demonstrated that it is possible to deliver good quality reparative interventions that conform to current best practice standards, particularly where the local service provider is experienced in the field of mediation and reparation. Those responsible for commissioning external service providers on a competitive basis were convinced that such an arrangement delivered better value for money and generated a greater range of innovative practices, though in the absence of a rigorous cost effectiveness study it is difficult to verify these claims.

The final 'mixed economy' model was based on a hybrid between the other two and involved an employee from a voluntary sector organisation (for example a mediation and reparation scheme) being seconded to work within a YOT, while the organisation itself was contracted to assist in the delivery of reparative interventions. The potential advantage offered by this model is that it should achieve many of the benefits associated with the in-house approach, including better communications and a more integrated approach, even in areas where suitably trained criminal justice practitioners are not available. These benefits are only likely to be fully attainable, however, where seconded staff are fully and effectively integrated into the rest of the YOT, and where appropriate and effective victim consultation procedures are in place. Unfortunately, the only pilot area to adopt this approach experienced difficulties on both counts, since relations were strained between different members of the reparation team, and the victim consultation procedure was seriously defective. These difficulties were attributable to 'local' factors, however, and were not systemic. Under different circumstances a hybrid model should be capable of operating very effectively.

Quite apart from the 'structural' arrangements that were put in place for delivering reparative interventions, the implementation of the new measure also presented a number of major operational challenges. The most important of these relate to the training of YOT and court staff, the need to develop a new youth justice culture within the multidisciplinary teams, and the need for effective partnerships between YOTs and courts, based on the distinctive ethos (see above) that underpins the Act.

Training was a major issue within the pilot YOTs themselves, and the emphasis given to training in the non-pilot areas has been given an increasingly high profile by the Youth Justice Board. However, training for magistrates was highly variable within the pilot areas, in terms of both quality and quantity. This was reflected in the lack of a shared understanding on the part of courts, YOT practitioners and external contract staff in some of the pilot areas as to what reparation is and the way the orders should be used. Although there was evidence that the pilot YOTs themselves had largely succeeded in building effective and coherent multidisciplinary teams and were beginning to develop a distinctive new youth justice culture, there was much less evidence of a corresponding change on the part of magistrates. Moreover, the need for appropriate training of magistrates in non-pilot areas may be even more acute, given the competing contemporaneous demand for intensive training with regard to the implementation in October 2000 of the 1998 Human Rights Act.

Reparation order evaluation: key findings

Take-up patterns

The pilot evaluation recorded the numbers of each new order (reparation order, action plan order, parenting order and child safety order, plus the final warnings that are delivered by the police) within each pilot area. Of the three principal court-based orders the most numerous were reparation orders (1,232), followed by action plan orders (841) and parenting orders (85)[9]. The great majority of reparation orders (60%) came from a single pilot area (Wessex). Sheffield contributed 22 per cent of the total, Wolverhampton accounted for 14 per cent, and the three West London YOTs provided just 6 per cent of the total. These figures suggest that the take-up pattern for the reparation order was highly variable in the different pilot areas.

Unfortunately it is not possible to determine precisely the proportionate use of each of the new disposals relative to existing sentencing options. The Crime and Criminal Justice Unit at the Home Office which is responsible for monitoring sentencing disposals did not allocate separate codes for each new order, but simply required them to be recorded collectively as 'otherwise dealt with'. However, it is possible to use these figures to determine the approximate combined 'market share' for the three new disposals, the majority of which, as we have seen, consisted of reparation orders.[10] This analysis confirms that there were indeed striking variations in the level of take-up for the new orders, which in three of the pilots fluctuated between 25 per cent and as high as 50 per cent of all sentences imposed on offenders within the relevant age groups, while they scarcely made any impact at all in the three London YOTs.[11]

It is difficult to account for the exceedingly low take-up of the new orders in general, and reparation orders[12] in particular, in London, compared with other pilot areas. One tentative explanation (based on the admittedly limited number of interviews we conducted) is that the differences of opinion between magistrates and the (external) service providers with regard to the nature of reparation and the way it should be used may have been more pronounced in London than elsewhere. If so, this lack of a shared understanding may have contributed to a reluctance on the part of magistrates to make reparation orders. An additional, related factor is that the victim consultation provisions may have been interpreted more strictly in London than elsewhere. Thus, in London it seemed to be widely assumed that if victims had not been consulted by the time an offender was due to be sentenced, reparation of any kind would be inappropriate, whereas elsewhere offenders were often ordered to undertake some form of community reparation in such circumstances.

Profile of offenders and offences in cases involving reparation orders

The evaluation examined a total of 602 reparation order case file records (approximately one in two of the total number imposed during the pilot period). The overwhelming majority of offenders were male (85%). The average age was 14.3 years, with a range from 10 to 18 years. Most offenders were recorded as white (73%), nine per cent were recorded as black, two per cent as Asian, and five per cent were from other ethnic backgrounds. (Of the remainder, the offender's ethnicity was unknown in a further three per cent of cases, and was not recorded in 8 per cent.) Just under two thirds of offenders were still in full-time education, though slightly more than one fifth were said to be unemployed. Two fifths of offenders lived with both parents, or a parent plus partner, and a slightly smaller proportion lived with just one parent. Some 8 per cent were in care and 5 per cent lived independently.

The great majority of offenders in receipt of a reparation order were convicted of a single, relatively minor offence. Just under half were convicted of offences involving theft or dishonesty. The remainder were fairly evenly split between offences involving criminal damage, offences relating to motor vehicles or violence (12–13% each) or disorder (8%). One in four cases involved co-defendants, most of whom (78%) were themselves young offenders. A slight majority (52%) had just one or two previous convictions, mostly for similar, relatively minor offences and chiefly dealt with by means of a caution or reprimand. Approximately one in six offenders had no previous cautions, warnings or convictions. This final statistic gives some credence to concerns expressed by several YOT practitioners that one effect of the Crime and Disorder Act may have been an increasing tendency to prosecute even minor offences in such circumstances, without going through the 'normal' pre-prosecution tariff.[13]

Police decisions as to the appropriate course of action are supposed to be based on the use of a formal, more objective, offence-based 'gravity' instrument, though there were some concerns about the way this was being used in the pilot areas. Just under half of all offenders who were given a reparation order had either no 'risk factors' or just one. The most frequently recorded risk factors related either to educational disaffection or problems in the young offender's home and family environment and, as such, present a potential challenge to those responsible for delivering indirect reparative interventions in particular, and also to the sentencers who impose them.

Reparation orders were most likely to be imposed following a new-style specific-sentence report (67%),[14] although one in four orders involved the use of a more traditional pre-sentence report. A verbal or other report was provided in four per cent of cases, and a reparation order was imposed without a report of any kind in a further four per cent of cases. In practice an offender's suitability for reparation is often based on a 'stand-down' report, which is compiled during a very brief court adjournment; but this affords very little time to undertake a proper assessment. In one or two case studies it was clear that this had resulted in a failure to identify factors that would have been relevant when passing sentence.

Profile of victims involved in reparation order cases

Information relating to the type of victims involved in reparation cases is summarised in Tables 5.1 and 5.2. Just under half of all cases involved either a single or multiple individual victims. However, there was considerable variation between the pilots, since the proportion of cases involving individual victims ranged from 28 per cent in one area to 52 per cent in another. The proportion of cases involving business or corporate victims averaged 39 per cent across all the pilots, and ranged between 31 and 46 per cent.

Table 5.1 Type of victim	
Single Individual	43%
Business or corporate victims	39%
Multiple individual victims	4%
No identifiable victim	10%
No information as to type of victim	4%

Table 5.2 Characteristics of individual victims	
Known to offender	26%
Victim gender	63% male
Victim age	27% under 17 65% 17–59
Victim race (where recorded)	80% white

The victim was known to the offender in just 26 per cent of all cases involving individual victims, two-thirds of whom were aged between 17 and 59.

Victim consultation procedures: implementation and impact

Pilot YOTs varied considerably in the type of victim consultation policies and procedures they adopted,[15] and also in their effectiveness. Victims were said to have been consulted in two-thirds of all reparation cases with identifiable victims, which is lower than might have been expected.

One reason for the relatively high rate of non-consultation may have been a reluctance to contact victims if the offender's attitude appeared negative or hostile at the time of assessment. One or two pilot YOTs had a policy of not even attempting to consult with victims in such cases for fear of re-victimising them. They appear to have taken the view that it is better not to raise unrealistic expectations on the part of victims if a mediated outcome does not seem feasible, presumably because there is no realistic prospect of 're-empowering' them.

Although the concern to avoid revictimisation is laudable it can also – paradoxically – result in victims' interests being treated as of secondary importance. By adopting a policy of non-consultation in such cases, some of the pilot YOTs appear to have assumed (contrary to the evidence) that victims are only interested in direct reparation and are unlikely to derive any benefit from being consulted if direct reparation is not feasible. Not all victims are interested in the prospect of meeting or receiving direct reparation from their offender, however, though they may still wish to express a view on the subject of community reparation in such cases. They may also wish to be kept informed of the outcome.

A second and rather less laudable explanation for the relatively high rate of non-consultation involved a degree of cultural resistance on the part of some YOT workers who were reluctant to accept that their responsibilities also included addressing the needs of victims. One of the pilot YOTs adopted the commendable practice of routinely monitoring compliance with its victim consultation policy by auditing all pre-sentence reports. These disclosed that full compliance was as low as 25 per cent in some areas, and that some YOT staff (particularly those who had come from more traditional youth justice backgrounds) openly refused to contact victims because they did not consider it to be part of their job.

Of those victims who were consulted, exactly half indicated that they were willing for their offender to undertake some form of reparation. Just under two-thirds of those who consented agreed to accept some form of direct reparation, and just over one-third agreed that their offender should perform some kind of indirect reparation. Once again there were pronounced variations between the pilots, both with regard to their victim response rates, and also in respect of the proportion of victims who were willing to accept direct reparation of some kind, as opposed to indirect reparation.

The victim response rate (percentage of victims contacted who agreed to some form of reparation) ranged from a low of only 20 per cent in one pilot area to a high of 75 per cent in another. Likewise, the proportion of victims who were willing to receive direct reparation ranged from just over half (53%) to over 90 per cent. These variations were almost certainly attributable to the different consultation procedures adopted by the different pilot YOTs. The least effective method consisted of a standard letter (written on YOT headed notepaper), which required victims to make contact with the YOT if they wished to accept some form of reparation or find out more about it. The highest rates of victim participation were associated with much more pro-active forms of consultation, in which the initial contact (either by letter or telephone call) was followed up by a visit or telephone call, unless victims indicated that they did not wish to be involved.

The consultation-related shortcomings described so far mainly relate to implementational problems, many of which could be avoided by improved training and procedures or monitoring and enforcement arrangements. However, a more 'systemic' problem that became more acute as the pilots progressed relates to the increasingly restrictive way in which the Data Protection Act 1998 is now being interpreted by the Home Office and other authorities, compared with the early days of the pilots. The effect of this interpretation is to put the onus on the police to identify the relevant victim(s) and obtain their consent before passing on their details to those who may be responsible for consulting victims on the subject of reparation. This raises concerns as to the willingness and ability of the police to determine the most appropriate victim in cases involving multiple or corporate victims. It also raises doubts as to whether they are the most appropriate agency to initiate the consultation process itself, as opposed to suitably trained and experienced staff who are employed (directly or indirectly) by the YOT.

Reparation orders and the courts

The main problem with regard to the implementation of reparation orders by the courts[16] related to the tension between two conflicting objectives of the Crime and Disorder Act: the requirement to consult with victims, which may frequently be time-consuming if done sensitively; and the speeding up of youth justice by reducing the time from arrest to sentence. None of the pilots was able to consult with victims routinely before the date of conviction, as envisaged by the original Home Office guidelines.

In some of the pilot areas, courts were prepared to grant adjournments of up to three weeks to enable consultations to be concluded. In other areas, however, magistrates (including stipendiaries) routinely refused to adjourn for this reason, insisting that offenders be sentenced on the day. For many sentencers it appeared that victim consultation was viewed as an optional extra that should only be tolerated where it does not hold up the proceedings. A much more constructive response was encouraged in one of the pilot areas in cases where consultation with a victim had not been concluded at the time of sentence. This required magistrates to be less prescriptive in stipulating the detailed content of an order. Instead, the order would authorise reparation workers to facilitate either an appropriate form of direct reparation with the named victim if the latter was agreeable, or an appropriate form of indirect reparation if no agreement was forthcoming. This makes it possible to consult with victims without pressurising them or hindering progress towards faster processing times for offenders. However, it also calls for a much more collaborative decision-making process, and a responsible approach on the part of reparation workers, both in facilitating the reparation and also in providing regular feedback to the courts.

As for the type of reparation orders imposed by the courts, the great majority (80%) of reparation orders were said to involve indirect reparation, and in 63 per cent of cases reparation was ordered to be made to the community.[17] About one in five cases resulted in reparation being undertaken for the benefit of a named person. Only 9 per cent of cases resulted in mediation between victim and offender, though the victim(s) received some form of direct reparation in a further 12 per cent of cases. The problems associated with the victim consultation procedures (see above) are likely to have boosted the proportion of cases involving indirect or community reparation.

Overall assessment

Reparation orders were favourably reviewed in general. Offenders agreed that they would have to put right the harm they had caused. Almost without exception, offenders felt that they had been treated fairly by reparation workers (in sharp contrast to the way some of them felt they had been treated by the police or the courts). Offenders' parents mostly appreciated the help provided by YOT and reparation workers, for which several said they had been crying out for years. Many felt that the reparation order had been helpful in keeping their youngsters off the streets and productively occupied, but some complained that the orders themselves were too short.

Not all victims felt that their needs had been met by the reparation they received, and most felt that the offenders' interests had been seen as paramount. Nevertheless, the majority of victims who were interviewed were pleased to have been invited to take part in the process, and viewed it as a positive experience. Most took the view that getting offenders to meet their victims or provide direct reparation might help to discourage further offending, and for some victims it clearly had been a very positive experience. Magistrates' attitudes about reparation were more mixed. Some welcomed the fact that offenders were required to 'do something positive' instead of just being talked to, and felt that it was particularly appropriate for young offenders, but others regretted the demise of the conditional discharge and some expressed doubts about the extent to which victims' needs can be met, particularly with the emphasis on speeding up trial procedures, and in the absence of better resources. Some clearly viewed the reparation order in a much more punitive light than many reparation workers did.

Conclusions

The evaluation of the reparation order highlighted a number of implementational problems of the kind that any new criminal justice measure might be expected to give rise to. However, it also identified some more systemic problems – particularly in relation to the victim consultation process, and the way the reparation order is regarded and used by some magistrates – that will have to be tackled if the new order is to address the needs of victims while also seeking to address offenders' behaviour more constructively than in the past.

In relation to the criminal justice system as a whole, the evaluation confirms that while the reparation order has helped to establish some basic elements of a restorative justice approach as part of the mainstream response to youth offending behaviour for the first time, the context and manner in which it operates is still largely shaped by the traditional criminal justice process. The result has been the introduction of a hybrid form of justice that is neither purely restorative nor purely retributive, but incorporates elements of both approaches.

Notes

1. These and other restorative justice processes are described more fully in Marshall (1999) and Dignan and Lowey (2000).
2. These other types of reparative interventions are not discussed in detail here, but see Dignan (1999) and, for the results of the national evaluation referred to below, see Holdaway *et al.* (2001); Dignan *et al.* (forthcoming).
3. The pilot areas comprised the three London Boroughs of Hammersmith and Fulham, Kensington and Chelsea and the City of Westminster; also Sheffield, Wolverhampton and Wessex, which comprises Hampshire and the unitary authorities of Southampton, Portsmouth and the Isle of Wight. Other areas were also selected to pilot limited aspects of the Crime and Disorder Act, such as the parenting order and child safety order. These are referred to in the national evaluation reports as 'partial pilot sites', but are not featured here.

4. The law governing the reparation order is now contained in the consolidating Powers of Criminal Courts (Sentencing) Act 2000 Chapter VI, sections 73–5 inc. See for details Ashworth 2000; Cavadino and Dignan 2001.

5. Two interim reports were produced, the first of which (Hine *et al.* 1999) is available on the Home Office web site. See Holdaway *et al.* (2001)

6. In respect of each of the measures, five cases were selected from each of the four main pilot areas. Where possible, each of these case studies was based on interviews with the young offender, parents, YOT workers and other relevant personnel involved in the delivery of the measures, and also victims, where appropriate.

7. The Youth Justice Board was set up by the Crime and Disorder Act to monitor the operation of the youth justice system, advise on how the principal aim of preventing youth offending might best be pursued, and promote the development of good practice. Part way through the piloting process, the board established a number of 'pathfinder' YOTs in order to identify good practice lessons for others. See Holdaway *et al.* 2001, p.48 for comment.

8. See Hine *et al.* 1999 for an early evaluation of the creation and development of the YOTs themselves, including their composition, governance and funding arrangements.

9. A further 199 parenting orders were imposed in the partial pilot sites referred to in Note 3 above. The Crime and Disorder Act also introduced a fourth order, the Child Safety Order, but only two of these were imposed, both in partial pilots.

10. The number of cases recorded as 'otherwise dealt with' in each of the pilot areas was negligible prior to the introduction of the new measures.

11. In London the 'otherwise dealt with' category averaged just 2.75 per cent over the life of the pilots, compared with 1.1 per cent before the pilots started.

12. The London pilots were unique in imposing considerably more action plan orders than reparation orders.

13. Consisting of a new-style 'reprimand', followed by a 'final warning' and then prosecution. The subsequent introduction of a mandatory referral for offenders who have not previously been prosecuted (and who intend to plead guilty) to a youth offender panel effectively adds another tier to the process.

14. These shorter and more focused reports were intended to be used in place of the more comprehensive and time-consuming pre-sentence report in cases thought to be suitable for either a reparation order or an action plan order.

15. For further details see Dignan 2000.

16. There were other implementational problems in some pilot areas, which highlighted the need for more and better training. There were cases, for example, in which magistrates unilaterally increased the amount of direct reparation an offender was to perform without regard to the victim's own stated preferences; or sought an apology from an offender who had pleaded not guilty and continued at the time of sentence to deny any responsibility for harming the victim.

17. In one of the pilot areas (the one with the 'opt-in' consultation procedure), the proportion of cases resulting in community reparation was as high as 85 per cent. This high level of community reparation fuelled criticism (not confined to this particular pilot) that the reparation order was frequently being used as a form of junior community service order.

References

Ashworth A. (2000) *Sentencing and Criminal Justice*. London: Butterworths.

Cavadino M. and Dignan J. (1997) *The Penal System: An Introduction*. Second edition. London: Sage.

Cavadino M. and Dignan J. (2001) *The Penal System: An Introduction*. Third edition. London: Sage.

Dignan J. (1999) 'The Crime and Disorder Act and the prospects for restorative justice.' *Criminal Law Review,* January, 48–60.

Dignan J. (2000) *Youth Justice Pilots Evaluation: Interim Report on Reparative Work and Youth Offending Teams.* London: Home Office. See also Home Office website: www.homeoffice.gov.uk/cpd/jou/jou.htm

Dignan J. with Kerri Lowey (2000) *Restorative Justice Options for Northern Ireland: A Comparative Review. Research Report No. 10.* Belfast: The Stationery Office for the Review of Criminal Justice in Northern Ireland.

Dignan J., Davidson N., Holdaway S. and Marsh P. with Hammersley R. and Hine, J. (forthcoming)) *Labour's Youth Offending Teams: Charting a New Course for Juvenile Justice?* Winchester: Waterside Press.

Hine J., Davidson N., Dignan J., Hammersley R., Holdaway S. and Marsh P. (1999) *Youth Justice Pilots Evaluation: First Interim Report on Youth Offending Teams, April, 1999.* See Home Office web site: www.homeoffice.gov.uk/cpd/jou/jou.htm

Holdaway S., Davidson N., Dignan J., Hammersley R., Hine J. and Marsh P. (2001) *Youth Justice Pilots Evaluation: Final Report.* RDS occassional paper No. 69. London: Home Office.

Marshall T. F. (1999) *Restorative Justice: An Overview.* London: HMSO.

Morris A. and Gelsthorpe L. (2000), 'Something old, something blue, something borrowed, but something new?' *Criminal Law Review,* 18–30.

Victim Support (1999) *Restorative Justice and the Crime and Disorder Act.* Paper produced for the Victim Support National Conference, 17 June 1999.

Williams B. (2000) 'Victims of crime and the new youth justice.' In B. Goldson (ed.) *The New Youth Justice.* Lyme Regis: Russell House.

Youth Justice Board (2000) *Guidance on Developing Restorative Practice with Young Offenders and Victims of Crime.* London: Youth Justice Board and Crime Concern.

6.

Responding to Victims of Crime in Rural Areas

Susan R. Moody[1]

Introduction

Victims of crime in rural areas represent a group that is often overlooked, both in victimological research and in practice development. This chapter aims to go some way towards closing that gap. It considers the problems faced by crime victims in the countryside and looks at ways of improving services to such victims. The analysis is based on three different sources: research findings from other studies of rural victimisation; a survey of Community Safety Strategies prepared by 14 Scottish local authorities designated as 'rural'; and the results from a questionnaire completed by relevant agencies in those 14 authorities. It also, where appropriate, draws on the author's own experience of working in victim support, first as director of Victim Support Scotland, more recently as chair of a local service, and currently as a board member of a new Scottish charity supporting the survivors of child sexual abuse.

Neglect of rural issues in criminology and victimology

Criminology owes its development as an academic discipline to the growth of cities and it is therefore not surprising that its focus has tended to be on urban society. By the 1900s the 'social problem' of crime was viewed predominantly as an urban issue in spite of clear evidence of rural unrest and disorder in Victorian times. Recorded crime rates throughout the last century supported this and still do today. Victim surveys, which produce data on unreported crime, also reveal clear differences between victimisation rates in rural and in urban areas. The most recent Scottish crime survey, for instance, shows that agricultural communities (Group C of the Scottish (ACORN)[2] classification) had the lowest risk of victimisation or of revictimisation across all crime categories included in the survey (MVA 1998). The prevalence of victimisation for household crime in such areas was 5.6 per cent compared with 14.1 per cent in less well-off council estates (*ibid.* Appendix A3.3). The same picture emerges in England and Wales, with households in rural areas being one of the lowest risk categories for burglary (Mirrlees-Black *et al.* 1998, p.iv). In relation to personal victimisation the differences are also significant, with a 1.3 per cent prevalence rate in agricultural areas compared with 5.6 per cent in the poorest council estates in Scotland (MVA 1998, Appendix A3.3). The most recent British crime survey cites living in rural areas as a key factor in reducing the risk of violence (Mirrlees-Black *et al.* 1998, p.vi).

The emergence of victimology and victim studies also reflected this urban focus, with Crime Surveys concentrating on victimisation in cities – for instance, the London borough of Islington (Crawford *et al.* 1990), Edinburgh (Anderson *et al.* 1990) and Merseyside (Kinsey 1984). An exception to this is the Aberystwyth Crime Survey, conducted in a university town situated in a predominantly rural area of mid-Wales (Koffman 1999). The early British crime surveys only covered the more heavily populated areas of England and until 1993 the equivalent Scottish crime survey was confined to the central belt of Scotland.

Developing victim support services in rural areas

Developments designed to assist crime victims also derived their impetus from the experience of victims in urban areas. The first Victim Support service in England began in Bristol and the first Women's Aid Refuge was established in London. Not surprisingly the headquarters for these organisations, as with most voluntary sector agencies, continue to be located in cities. Victim Support (VS) extended its coverage in a remarkably short space of time, so that between 1979 and 1987 the number of services increased by almost 900 per cent, from 34 to 305 (Rock 1990, p.213). However, it has taken much longer to establish Victim Support Services in more remote rural areas. In Scotland, there is still no service in Shetland, for instance, and in England and Wales the last service to be established was on the Isle of Man.

The practice model upon which all such services are based is very much designed for victims in urban areas. Victim Support Services, certainly in Scotland, were envisaged as very locally based, covering small geographic areas and encompassing one community. This was a deliberate policy to encourage volunteers and victims to identify with their area and to ensure a response that would reflect local circumstances. It was well suited to urban areas, where housing estates might be next door to each other but very clearly saw themselves as separate and distinctive communities. It was not, however, as well adapted to the situation in more sparsely populated areas where communities could extend over hundreds of miles. In addition, the original model for victim support required swift initial intervention, involving face-to-face contact with the crime victim within 24 hours of receipt of the referral, and a limited commitment thereafter, with other agencies taking over responsibility. This may have been an unrealistic ideal even in urban Victim Support Services confined to small geographical areas; it was impossible to implement in many rural areas.

Apart from the logistical difficulties caused by distance and physical isolation there were key cultural issues that I encountered in trying to develop Victim Support Services in rural Scotland in the 1980s. First, we faced greater resistance from criminal justice agencies towards the service, which was seen as unnecessary, both because of low crime levels and as the result of rural police officers' views of their own key role in supporting victims of crime. In one rural area it took a break-in at the home of the assistant chief constable's mother before it was possible to set up a local Victim Support Services. It was only then that this senior officer acknowledged the impact that crime can have on rural victims and accepted that the police might not be the most appropriate agency to provide such a service.

Second, local communities sometimes saw VS personnel as interfering – and urban – busybodies who did not understand their way of life. Rural crime victims, it was claimed, were best looked after by their families and neighbours. In any case, country people were felt to be better equipped to deal with crisis situations, being tougher and more resilient than city people. Of course victim support was a necessity in urban areas but not in the countryside.

Third, there was a problem with unreported victimisation which made it more difficult to reach crime victims. Evidence from Crime Surveys suggests that victims in rural areas are less likely to report crime, and that there may be increased pressures from their communities not to do so. (See, for instance, Anderson 1997, p.27.)

Fourth, there were problems about choosing the location for services in rural areas. Where there were villages or small towns of a similar size it could prove difficult to select the most appropriate one. The eventual choice might alienate potential volunteers and useful allies, such as local councillors.

In Scotland today Victim Support Services are organised to conform to local authority boundaries, of which there are 32. Each local authority can cover very diverse communities and a large geographic area. The Highlands authority, for instance, covers an area of over 10,000 square miles and includes within its boundaries the city of Inverness, which has the fastest growing population of any Scottish city, and about half a dozen large towns. But it also has the lowest overall population density of any region of the European Union. The Western Isles has no sizeable centres of population but covers at least a dozen populated islands. It has an ageing population, and the highest emigration rates of any part of the United Kingdom. Victim Support Services can and do take account of local differences in their internal structures, for example by encouraging the development of local volunteer groups that deal with referrals for one part of the local authority district only. However, it remains the case that models of service delivery that may be very suitable for urban areas cannot simply be transplanted to the countryside, particularly to remote areas. (For a discussion about community work in rural areas see Francis and Henderson 1992.)

Rural myths and realities

It is clear, then, that criminology and victimology in the United Kingdom have largely ignored the rural dimension to crime and victimisation. A similar trend is evident in the operation of Victim Support. However, it is also fair to add that this failure to differentiate the rural from the urban experience may in fact be an accurate reflection of 'real life', in that it has been asserted by some criminologists that differences between crime victims in the countryside and those in the city no longer exist. Given such key factors as globalisation, inmigration and the marginalisation of farming and other traditional rural occupations, it is claimed that the countryside has lost its distinctive character (see, for instance, the discussion in Anderson 1997). It is certainly true that crime trends and the nature of crime are broadly similar right across the United Kingdom. And it appears to be the case that the countryside is becoming more like the city, with victimisation rates rising in rural areas.

A further argument presented by critics of the 'rural', particularly geographers and rural sociologists, is that it does little to assist informed debate. Critics quite rightly assert that there is no homogenous countryside; the rural encompasses an enormous variety of physical and human geographies. While location is highly significant, a simple binary urban/rural divide cannot do justice to the diverse and complex differences contained in the 'rural'. Just as there is no one 'city' reality and crime rates can differ from street to street, neither is there one rural setting. In any case, the definition of what constitutes 'rural' is very much contested territory, with no clear consensus emerging. In Scotland it is usually based on population density at local authority level, and rural authorities are those with an average population density of less than one person per hectare. This includes authorities with large towns and some densely populated areas, such as North Ayrshire and

Stirling, and also very remote, thinly populated districts, such as the Western Isles. A definition which is frequently used in England makes the parish its focus and defines parishes with less than 10,000 people as rural (Rural Development Commission 1992).

Some would argue, then, that 'rural' is not a useful category because its use leads either to false dichotomies or to enforced homogeneity. This argument does not, however, account for the differences which undoubtedly do exist between urban and rural crime rates, neither does it explain other significant divergences between the city and the countryside in relation to, for example, levels of fear of crime, assessment of risk, and the prioritising of crime as a serious problem. These are clearly shown in studies conducted in rural areas of Scotland, Wales and England. (For detailed analysis of the position in all three countries and also in the Irish Republic see Dingwall and Moody 1999.) Anderson's work, for instance, demonstrates that the countryside continues to be a much safer place than the city, with analyses of police-recorded crime statistics showing four crimes in urban areas for every one committed in a rural area (Anderson 1997, Table 2). According to Anderson, crime is not perceived as a major problem in the countryside; indeed the safety of rural communities is regarded as a great advantage by those who live there. In his study respondents did express concern about specific problems which were crime-related, notably drug and alcohol misuse and petty vandalism. However, of far more concern to rural residents was lack of public transport, local employment opportunities and leisure facilities. Catriona Mirrlees-Black comes to similar conclusions in her review of rural crime data from three British Crime Surveys (Mirrlees-Black 1998).

Nevertheless, a recent study with a rural development focus, *Tackling Crime in Rural Scotland* (Smyth 1999), draws attention to features in the rural landscape which may make criminal victimisation more likely or more traumatic. The researcher's findings suggest that commercial premises, including village shops, working farms, and leisure facilities such as golf clubs and club huts, may be less well protected, more isolated, and therefore more vulnerable in rural areas and that repeat victimisation may be more likely in the countryside because of the absence of crime prevention measures. Travelling criminals pose particular difficulties because, with good road networks, they can access rural settlements easily and withdraw from them quickly. This study also notes the problems which ethnic minorities may face following criminal victimisation, arising out of their small numbers and cultural isolation. In England and Wales a useful practical guide to rural crime prevention (Husain 1995) comes to similar conclusions about the 'pernicious' consequences of crime in rural areas. An English study of the rural idyll attempts to puncture some of the myths about rural crime (Derounian 1993). The author notes the problems rural victims face because of physical isolation, transport problems to access services, and the closed nature of some rural communities which discourages reporting. Where perpetrators are known to each other there are more likely to be tensions and stress, he claims, especially for the victim.

A Scottish survey looking specifically at domestic abuse uncovered some interesting data on the experience of rural victims. Lack of access to information about services, poor or no emergency provision, limited choice and availability of support services, both statutory and voluntary, problems in securing privacy and maintaining confidentiality, and perceived 'tolerance' of domestic abuse all made things more difficult for women in rural areas. Staff providing services in such areas were more likely to have insufficient resources and less likely to receive appropriate training (Henderson 1997). These finding were replicated in an American study of rural Kentucky where physical isolation combined with a culture which accepts patriarchy resulted in major difficulties for battered women (Websdale 1998).

Apart from these studies, information derived from Crime Surveys and some practical guidance offered by groups like Crime Concern (Husain 1995) there is little original material from the United Kingdom about rural victimisation. Williams provides an excellent review of current literature (Williams 1999) and there has been some useful work on racist victimisation in rural areas (Henderson and Kaur 1999; NCVO 2000). However, for in-depth empirical studies of rural victimisation it is necessary to go further afield, to the United States and Australia. A particularly useful study was conducted in a rural area of New South Wales in 1989 (O'Connor and Gray 1989). The authors note the power of rural myths in reducing feelings of fear and modifying assessments of risk. They also underline the huge social changes taking place in the countryside which have influenced perceptions of the countryside and rural lifestyles. A more recent study by the Attorney General's Department of South Australia noted some significant differences between urban and rural victims. Rural victims were less likely to receive information about or to be referred to victim support or to be given advice on avoidance of repeat victimisation (South Australia Justice Department 2000, p.70).

Criminology and victimology in the United Kingdom have contributed relatively little research to enhance our understanding of rurality and its meaning for victims. Fortunately, rural geographers and sociologists in the United Kingdom have done much valuable work in deconstructing rural mythologies and their effect, not only on individual perceptions of the rural but also on the delivery of services in rural areas (Moody 1999). Beginning with Howard Newby in the 1970s such studies have offered us very useful and thought-provoking analyses of the potency of the rural ideal/idyll (Newby 1979). More recently Cloke and his colleagues have carried out some challenging studies in England and Wales (Cloke *et al.* 1997) and Shucksmith has explored the rural reality of Scottish communities where social exclusion is present but hidden (Shucksmith 2000). This work strongly supports the view that rurality is still of vital significance in shaping the way both town and country dwellers view their lives and also how they live them.

Studies of responses to criminal victimisation in rural areas

In order to collect data on the difficulties experienced by victims in rural areas and to obtain information on good practice in responding to victims in the countryside, a small-scale research study was conducted in the autumn of 2000.

1. Community safety strategies

The research began with an analysis of community safety strategies (CSSs), which all local authorities in Scotland have published or are currently compiling. The Scottish Executive's policy statement *Safer Communities in Scotland* (Scottish Executive 1999) began the process of developing CSSs at local level. It 'accepted that the most effective community strategies are based on locally defined information, needs and concerns' (*ibid.* p.1) and noted the problems in developing successful partnerships for community safety which the Audit Commission for England and Wales revealed, including weaknesses in reflecting local people's priorities and a lack of evidence-based strategies (Audit Commission 1999). The statement referred specifically to the development of rural policy generally by the new Scottish Executive, which has included the designation of 14 local authorities as 'rural' (Scottish Executive 2000a). The policy statement was followed by an Accounts Commission report on community safety partnerships in Scotland, *Safe and Sound*, published in May 2000, which made recommendations about future developments, including partnership working (Accounts Commission 2000). However, it should be noted that the situation in Scotland is not as far advanced as in England and Wales and there is no statutory requirement to devise and implement such policies, unlike the position in England and Wales under Section 6 of the Crime and Disorder Act 1998.

The models used in Scotland do, nevertheless, draw heavily on work already undertaken in England and Wales, and emphasis is placed on 'locally-appropriate structures, supported by systems and protocols' (Audit Commission 2000). A recent report on five local authorities chosen to assist in the development of a 'model of excellence' as 'pathfinders' suggests that progress across Scotland is patchy (Scottish Executive 2000b). Two of the five local authorities included in this evaluation were rural. In designing a CSS emphasis was placed on responding to local issues and on mainstreaming community safety into local and national policy, but there was no specific acknowledgement of any particular difficulties that might arise in rural areas. Perhaps this is not surprising, given the much lower rates of crime in rural areas. But it does suggest that the increased significance accorded by the Scottish Parliament to rural issues has not been reflected in policy initiatives across the board. Given that CSSs are required by the Scottish Executive to reflect local circumstances, it seems unfortunate that the use of CCTV in a large town is given in official guidance as an example of ways in which rural areas can tackle crime.

An analysis of the CSSs produced by the 14 Scottish rural local authorities demonstrates that most, though not all, refer to the needs of crime victims for support, and most pay particular attention to victims of domestic abuse. The Scottish Executive has made domestic abuse a major priority (Henderson 2000) and several of the CSSs make reference to developments in this area. For instance, in two local authorities outreach workers have been appointed to deal with cases in the more remote rural areas. Several CSSs also note the particular needs of victims of racist or homophobic crime. However, very few explicitly refer to the particular difficulties which victims in rural areas may face. According to one CSS:

> The historical perception would tend to place community value on safety topics in the more urban/built environment context where problems could potentially be anticipated and 'designed out' of any final scheme of things. (Argyll and Bute CSS)

It is striking, then, that while rural issues currently command far more time and energy at all levels of government in Scotland, this is not, for the most part, reflected in the CSSs of rural authorities.

2. Problems confronting victims of crime in rural areas

A questionnaire was sent to local authorities, police, victim support agencies (Victim Support and Women's Aid), prosecutors and sheriff clerks in the 14 rural local authorities, asking for their views on the problems confronting victims of crime living in rural areas and possible solutions to these difficulties. The response rate from the police and from local authorities was very good, with virtually all returning a completed questionnaire. There was a satisfactory return of about 50 per cent from victim support agencies but virtually no responses from prosecutors and sheriff clerks. These two agencies have not usually involved themselves in the design of CSSs, although efforts have been made in some local authorities to include them. It may be assumed from the very low response rate that prosecutors and sheriff clerks considered the issues contained in the questionnaire to be of no relevance to them. This is, perhaps, an unfortunate finding for victims in rural areas, when previous research has shown that the rural context of criminal justice can create particular difficulties (Harding and Williams 1994).

GEOGRAPHICAL ISOLATION

According to our respondents, crime victims in rural areas may have problems in obtaining a swift response from the police. Increasingly, local stations have closed and police officers are concentrated in towns and cities. In the Highlands of Scotland, for instance, it is not unusual for the nearest staffed police station to be 70 or more miles away. The Northern Constabulary covers an area similar in size to Belgium. Even where there is a local police presence it is unlikely to be staffed outside office hours and sometimes police officers are available there only a few hours a week. To ensure a response, phone calls to local stations are re-routed to the main centres, for instance Inverness and Dundee. This means that a victim will be able to report the crime but that officers may be required to come long distances, especially when the call is made at night or at weekends. The officers who arrive at the scene may not know the area and that may cause difficulties in finding isolated residences. Force service standards do stipulate normal response times in rural areas – for instance, in one force area the response rate within cities and towns with a staffed police station is 10 minutes and 20 minutes in rural areas. However, this would simply not be possible in other rural areas where distances are larger. (The Rural White Paper for England notes that in the Lancashire Police Authority the response time is 15 minutes in both urban and rural areas and that 'positive improvement in this aspect of police performance' is expected (DETR 2000, 4.5.8).)

In addition, other forms of immediate assistance, such as medical care, are unlikely to be directly accessible, and practical assistance, such as emergency repairs, may be hard to obtain quickly. The Rural White Paper sets as part of its Rural Services Standard a target of guaranteed access to a primary healthcare professional within 24 hours and to a doctor within 48 hours, to be achieved throughout England by 2004 (DETR 2000, Chapter 2).

Geographical distance also creates difficulties for victim support agencies. It is not usually possible for services in remote rural areas to provide a face-to-face response within 24 hours. Generally phone contact is established first and a suitable time fixed. This problem is compounded by a lack of volunteers in such areas and may also be affected by concerns about volunteers' safety.

Respondents made some useful suggestions about ways of dealing with geographical isolation. Police forces sometimes make use of special constables and retired personnel to assist in the more inaccessible rural areas. Remote reporting, where victims report to an agency other than the police, has been used successfully in cases of racist crime and homophobic criminal behaviour (Corteen *et al.* 2000). Voluntary and statutory agencies that are based in rural areas (in local schools, village halls, churches) or organisations that visit rural sites on a regular basis (including health visitors) could be used as initial reporting stations. Recruitment campaigns for victim support volunteers need to be targeted to ensure adequate coverage of geographically dispersed regions. The use of mobile phones by volunteers could make victim contact easier and increase safety.

ACCESS TO SERVICES FOR CRIME VICTIMS

Many respondents spoke about the urban model that is used in the location and structure of services of all kinds in rural areas. Their concern is reflected in some useful research on the delivery of health and social care services in rural areas (Barnes and Gould 1997). This study noted the 'widespread, but unfounded belief that mainstream planning automatically addresses the needs of people in rural areas, particularly if the county sees itself as generally "rural"'. (*ibid.* p.7). There is a need, according to this research, 'to persuade senior officers to take rural issues seriously' (*ibid.* p.25) and to 'accept rural communities face different challenges to urban areas' (*ibid.* p.46). Services, whether statutory or voluntary, tend to be centralised in towns. Available resources, such as village halls and local networks, are often not utilised to the full. These difficulties are also highlighted in the recent Rural White Paper for England (DETR 2000).

According to our respondents, victims may have to travel many miles to reach the nearest Victim Support office or Women's Aid refuge. Other services which victims may require, such as health and social services, are not always available close to home. There are particular difficulties in providing specialist services in rural areas, where economies of scale and small numbers may make such provision very expensive. Changes to local government introduced into Scotland in 1995 meant that each of the 32 local authorities became responsible for social services, whereas hitherto there had been only eight service providers. The result was that certain specialist services ceased to be available in the more rural authorities after that time, since the small client base in these areas inflated the cost of 'in-house' provision considerably. (For the position in relation to criminal justice social work services see Brown *et al.* 1998, p.13.) The situation has now improved somewhat with smaller local authorities 'buying in' outside expertise and combining with neighbouring authorities to offer specialist services.

In addition, access to criminal justice can undoubtedly present difficulties for some victims in rural areas. The nearest prosecutor's office and the closest sheriff court could be many miles away. While travel and subsistence expenses are paid, loss of earnings reimbursed and child care expenses met, the travelling time required for victims making statements or giving evidence may be considerable. The Rural White Paper notes the importance of technology in reducing the need for travel to courts, including the use of video-conferencing for witnesses in criminal trials (DETR 2000, Chapter 2).

Our respondents also felt that service delivery in rural areas can be very rigid and inflexible. For instance, a Women's Aid Co-ordinator noted a mindset among social workers that 'Tuesday is the day I visit so problems will have to be kept till then'. A lack of inter-agency work and a failure by statutory and voluntary agencies to share resources was perceived by some of our respondents as a major problem. The fact that key criminal justice agencies, the prosecutors and the sheriff clerks, did not see this survey as relevant to them suggests that all those organisations which have a role to play in assisting crime victims are not working together in a coordinated and, where appropriate, integrated way. Such multi-agency work is, of course, at the heart of community safety strategies, but is often difficult to implement in practice. (For a useful critique of the issues which can arise in multi-agency work on crime prevention and community safety see Hughes 1998.)

Concern was expressed by our respondents about a perceived failure on the part of central government to acknowledge the cost of service provision in rural areas. Per capita the costs of investigating crime and supporting victims of crime in rural areas are bound to be higher, particularly if face-to-face support is the preferred option. Respondents felt that this should be acknowledged in funding arrangements and that a rural premium should be awarded so that service funding could take account of geographical distance and other logistical difficulties. A recent analysis of health and community care services in Scotland suggests that

> The formula used to allocate resources between Health Boards in Scotland takes little account of the additional costs that are incurred in delivering healthcare in remote and rural areas of Scotland. (Scottish Executive 2000a, Chapter 4)

There was strong support for making services more accessible in rural areas, for example by sharing buildings in rural areas so that a variety of agencies could use them. Drop-in centres used by a variety of organisations to keep costs down and as locally based as possible were suggested. These recommendations for improving service provision are also put forward by Mary-Ann Smyth in her rural crime prevention guidance (Smyth 1999). She gives useful examples of old bank buildings or parts of tourist offices being used by the police and other agencies.

Some respondents were keen to stress the benefits of using technology to obtain information and to access services. The Rural White Paper also stresses the value of IT, promising that by 2005 all public services will be available on-line (DETR 2000, Chapter 2). Vulnerable victims, our respondents proposed, could be given mobile phones to keep them in touch with victim support agencies at all times. It was interesting that several of the police respondents suggested that a victims' helpline would be useful, without, apparently, knowing that such a facility already exists: the UK-wide Victim Supportline offers a service anywhere in the UK at local rates between 9am and 9pm Monday to Friday, 9am to 7pm Saturday and Sunday and 9am to 5pm on bank holidays. This should be more widely publicised so that all agencies involved in victim support are aware of it. Smyth notes a scheme for vulnerable people in remote areas, the Home Phone service, started by crime prevention panels in one rural authority. Volunteers phone such people each day to check that all is well.

Above all, respondents felt that responses needed to be flexible and to reflect the local community's needs rather than match some urban blueprint; what was needed was a 'local response to local needs and problems'. Some concern was expressed about ensuring that responses to crime victims in rural areas were realistic and acknowledged local difficulties, such as geographical isolation and patchy services. There was also a perception on the part of some respondents that more direction, guidance and a coherent strategy on service access and delivery were needed. Some local authorities are using community safety teams to develop knowledge and expertise locally and to feed local issues back to service providers and policy makers.

TRANSPORT

A major problem mentioned by almost all the respondents was public transport in rural areas. Services are infrequent and only available on certain routes, all of which are focused on towns. There is sometimes no synchronisation between different services, so that it is not possible to get from one place to another in the same day. In a survey of 4,500 people living in the

Highlands, Western Isles, Orkney and Shetland four out of ten said they were dissatisfied or very dissatisfied with local bus services (Northern Constabulary Community Consultation 1999, para. 2.12.3). This proportion increased to nearly 50 per cent in areas outside the main population centre of Inverness. The cost of petrol in rural areas is also significantly higher:

> The average price of a full tank of unleaded petrol in the Highlands and Islands [in summer 2000] was £54.24 compared to £49.74 in Edinburgh. But prices in more remote areas such as the Western isles and North West Sutherland were 12 to 15p a litre above the average for Inverness [the main town in the Highlands]. (*The Herald* 2.11.00, p.2)

Some helpful guidance on improving transport services in rural areas has been undertaken for the Scottish Executive. A combination of more flexible services, utilising, for instance, the school bus, postal van and other mobile units, could provide more economic services to rural residents. Encouraging car sharing through financial incentives has also been suggested. The price of petrol in rural areas could be targeted, since it not only makes access to services more problematic but also increases the cost of service provision significantly (Herbert 1996). The Rural White Paper has set a target for the population living within 10 minutes' walk of an hourly bus service to increase from 37 per cent to 50 per cent by 2010 (DETR 2000, Chapter 2).

CULTURAL ISSUES

Several of our respondents noted the cultural differences between the city and the countryside that influenced their work with victims of crime in rural areas.

'Us and them'
Our respondents were concerned about the cosy myths regarding rural life – myths that did not, in their experience, always reflect the reality of country life. The countryside is no longer populated solely or even mainly by people who share a common heritage and attachment to the land where they live. Increasingly, the indigenous population has been joined by a variety of other groups, most of which have no background in rural life. For many country

people these incomers can be divided into two groups – the desirable and the undesirable. The desirable include commuters, self-employed businesses, those seeking 'the good life', people who buy holiday homes in the country and retired people, including those in retirement and nursing homes. The undesirable encompass New Age travellers, DSS tenants and others whose lifestyles do not conform to the local norm, for instance, openly gay or lesbian couples. Even the desirable groups may find themselves severely socially isolated if they become victims of crime. If they have neighbours living close by they may have no links with them and there may be some hostility, because of perceived differences in income levels and a lack of shared understanding. This is compounded where the incomers are in the 'undesirable' category. So the close-knit community networks which people see in the countryside may be more imaginary than real for some crime victims.

Respondents agreed that it was unwise for criminal justice and support services to make assumptions about 'close-knit communities' and 'helpful neighbours' supporting victims in rural areas, something which they would not assume in urban areas. They felt that support must be given on an individual basis, responding to each particular victim's needs, and should not be based on stereotyping.

'We look after our own'

Crime rates are low in the countryside but the reporting of crime is also lower than in urban areas. This may be partly because of the difficulties in reporting crime, already noted above, but it also reflects an approach to disputes which encourages internal management of conflicts rather than official involvement. This may, of course, be laudable and echo Nils Christie's plea that conflicts be given back to those who created them (Christie 1977). But it also has a darker side, especially in relation to certain crimes, such as domestic abuse and sexual crimes. Research on responses to domestic abuse in Scotland has pointed up the particular problems which women in rural areas face. In a community where everyone knows everyone else's business, wife assault may be viewed as a reflection of the wife's shortcomings. Victims may be expected to 'put up with it' so as to maintain community solidarity.

Knowledge of and perhaps kinship with the perpetrator may make it more difficult for community members to acknowledge the harm done to the victim. He or she may be ostracised if the crime is reported.

'We can cope'

A further difficulty referred to by our respondents is the notion of self-reliance, which is seen by some to characterise country dwellers. Whereas city folk are expected to require help from outside, the tougher breed living in the country should be able to cope without outside help. One police officer noted that this 'rural sense of independence' could adversely affect victims who might be deterred from seeking help.

Everyone's business

Victims living in rural areas may, in spite of isolation and geographical distance, be much less anonymous to their neighbours and it may be difficult to keep sensitive matters private, including involvement with criminal justice agencies and with victim support. Where victims are also offenders this fact is likely to be well-known and therefore there may be a perception that they do not deserve support, on the part of the police as well as local people. Victim Support workers felt that particular care should be taken in allocating volunteers to rural referrals so that they do not deal with referrals on their doorstep. Very close attention needs to be paid to discussion of cases and to any personal knowledge on the volunteer's part regarding the criminal incident.

Agencies as 'outsiders'

Some respondents felt that people living in rural areas who did not have services immediately available to them in their locality perceived agencies such as Victim Support and Women's Aid as 'outsiders'. There could be a lack of confidence in the work of these agencies and a feeling that they knew nothing about the victims' community. This could deter rural victims from using these services. It was suggested that local professionals who already had credibility locally, such as the GP, health visitor or minister, should be given training to equip them to inform victims about victim support agencies and to assist victims themselves. Attention should also be given to advertising these services locally.

'It couldn't happen here'

Because crime is a rarer occurrence in rural areas, people may experience higher levels of fear and concern after victimisation. Respondents noted that rural crime victims may be 'less streetwise' than urban dwellers and therefore suffer more severely as the result of victimisation. They may also have fewer people with whom to share their experience. There may be greater fear of re-victimisation and fewer opportunities for preventive measures to be taken because of isolation.

Conclusion

The needs of victims of crime in rural areas require special consideration, given the particular problems that they face. Geographical isolation, difficulties accessing services, and cultural differences may all affect the provision of support to crime victims in the countryside. The increased pressure from rural residents to have their special circumstances acknowledged by central and local government may produce benefits for victim support in rural areas, encouraging it to respond in appropriate and flexible ways and providing additional resources to meet the needs of crime victims in rural areas.

> Our philosophy stems from concern for equal opportunity. When you plan services you must consider people's circumstances. 'Rurality' is one set of circumstances. (Barnes and Gould 1997, p.6)

Notes

1. My thanks to Andrew Mackenzie, Department of Law, University of Dundee, for his research assistance, and to a local charitable trust for contributing to the cost of the empirical work.
2. This classification, which is based on 100 variables from the 1991 census, segments Scottish housing into 43 types or 8 main groups.

References

Accounts Commission (2000) *Safe and Sound: A Study of Community Partnerships in Scotland.* Edinburgh: Audit Scotland.

Anderson S., Grove Smith C., Kinsey R. and Wood J. (1990) *The Edinburgh Crime Survey: First Report.* Edinburgh: Scottish Office Central Research Unit.

Anderson S. (1997) *A Study of Crime in Rural Scotland.* Edinburgh: Scottish Executive Central Research Unit.

Audit Commission (1999) *Safety in Numbers – Promoting Community Safety.* London: Audit Commission.

Audit Commission (2000) Community Safety Website www.audit-commission.uk/comsafe/1_0html).

Barnes L. and Gould J. (1997) *Strategies for Success in Rural Care.* London: NCVO.

Brown L., Levy L. and McIvor G. (1998) *Social Work and Criminal Justice Volume 3: The National and Local Context of Policy Implementation.* Edinburgh, Scottish Office Central Research Unit.

Christie N. (1977) 'Conflicts as property.' *British Journal of Criminology 17*, 1.

Cloke P., Goodwin M. and Milbourne P. (1997) *Rural Wales: Community and Marginalisation.* Cardiff: University of Wales Press.

Corteen K., Moran L., Skeggs B. and Tyrer P. (2000) *Citizens' Enquiry Reports: Lancaster and Manchester.* The ESRC Violence, Sexuality and Space Research Project. London: Birkbeck College, London University.

Crawford A., Jones T., Woodhouse T. and Young J. (1990) *Second Islington Crime Survey.* Middlesex: Middlesex Polytechnic.

Department of the Environment, Transport and Regions (DETR) (2000) *Our Countryside: The Future – A Fair Deal for Rural England.* Rural White Paper. London, DETR Cmnd 4909.

Derounian J. (1993) *Another Country: Real Life beyond Rose Cottage.* London: NCVO.

Dingwall G. and Moody S. R. (eds.) (1999) *Crime and Conflict in the Countryside.* Cardiff: University of Wales Press.

Francis D. and Henderson P. (1992) *Working with Rural Communities.* London: Macmillan.

Harding C. and Williams J. (eds.) (1994) *Legal Provision in the Rural Environment.* Cardiff: University of Wales Press.

Henderson P. and Kaur R. (1999) *Rural Racism in the UK. Examples of Community-based Responses.* London: Community Development Foundation.

Henderson S. (1997) *Service Provision to Women Experiencing Domestic Violence in Scotland.* Edinburgh: Scottish Office Central Research Unit.

Henderson S. (2000) *The Development of the Scottish Partnership on Domestic Abuse and Recent Work in Scotland.* Edinburgh: Central Research Unit, Scottish Executive.

Herbert S. (1996) *The Scottish Rural Transport Action Guide: Practical Advice on How to Address your Community's Transport Needs.* Edinburgh: Scottish Office Central Research Unit.

Hughes G. (1998) *Understanding Crime Prevention: Social Control, Risk and Late Modernity.* Buckingham: Open University Press.

Husain S. (1995) *Cutting Crime in Rural Areas: A Practical Guide for Parish Councils.* Swindon: Crime Concern.

Kinsey R. (1984) *Merseyside Crime Survey: First Report.* Liverpool: Merseyside County Council.

Koffman L. (1999) 'Crime in rural Wales.' In G. Dingwall and S. R. Moody (eds.) *Crime and Conflict in the Countryside.* Cardiff: University of Wales Press.

MVA (1998) *Main Findings from the 1996 Scottish Crime Survey.* Edinburgh: Scottish Office Central Research Unit.

Mirrlees-Black C. (1998) *Rural Areas and Crime: Findings from the British Crime Survey.* Research Findings No. 77. London: Home Office.

Mirrlees-Black C., Budd T., Partridge S. and Mayhew P. (1998) *The 1998 British Crime Survey: England and Wales.* Home Office Statistical Bulletin 21/98, London: Home Office.

Moody S. R. (1999) 'Rural neglect: The case against criminology.' In G. Dingwall and S. R. Moody (eds.) *Crime and Conflict in the Countryside.* Cardiff: University of Wales Press.

National Council for Voluntary Organisations (2000) *Rural Anti-racism Project Report.* London: NCVO.

Newby H. (1979) *Green and Pleasant Land? Social Change in Rural England.* London: Wildwood House.

Northern Constabulary (1999) *Northern Constabulary Community Consultation: Draft Report.* Inverness: Northern Constabulary.

O'Connor M. E. and Gray D. E. (1989) *Crime in a Rural Community.* Sydney: Federation Press.

Rock P. (1990) *Helping Victims of Crime: The Home Office and the Rise of Victim Support in England and Wales.* Oxford: Oxford University Press.

Rural Development Commission (1992) *Guidance on Developing a Rural Strategy.* London: Rural Development Commission.

Shucksmith M. with Philip L. (2000) *Social Exclusion in Rural Areas: Literature Review and Conceptual Framework.* Edinburgh: Scottish Executive Central Research Unit.

Smyth M. (1999) *Tackling Crime in Rural Scotland.* Edinburgh: Scottish Office Central Research Unit.

The Scottish Executive (1999) *Safer Communities in Scotland – Guidance for Community Safety Partnerships.* Edinburgh: Scottish Executive.

The Scottish Executive (2000a) *Towards a Development Strategy for Rural Scotland.* Edinburgh: Scottish Executive.

The Scottish Executive (2000b) *Threads of Success – A Study of Community Safety Partnerships in Scotland.* Edinburgh: Scottish Executive.

South Australia Justice Department (2000) *Victims of Crime Review Report Two: Survey of Victims of Crime.* Adelaide: Attorney-General's Department.

Websdale N. (1998) *Rural Woman Battering and the Justice System: an Ethnography.* Thousand Oaks and London: Sage.

Williams B. (1999) 'Rural victims of crime.' In G. Dingwall and S. R. Moody (eds.) *Crime and Conflict in the Countryside.* Cardiff: University of Wales Press.

7

Supporting Victims of Racist Abuse and Violence

Charlotte Knight and Karen Chouhan

Introduction

The 'Butetown Three'

> *On 19 August 1997, two young black students, Marcus Walters (18) and Francisco Borg (17) in Butetown, Cardiff, were on an errand for the mother of one of the young men. They had Marcus's little sister, Emma Walters (5), in the back of the car. A white man of skinhead appearance, on a bike, rode towards them, kicked the car and shouted abuse. Marcus stopped the car; as he got out the skinhead approached him and punched him. Another skinhead with a dog joined in; he opened the back door where Emma was sitting and began to threaten her with the dog.*
>
> *Marcus and Francisco were now shouting for someone to get the girl out of the car. A Bahranian student took the girl and shouted that he would meet them later in the Spar shop.*
>
> *Marcus and Francisco then quickly got back in the car to drive away. They drove around in a circle to try and get back to the Spar shop. However, some skins had also gone to the shop and chased the student and Emma out. On seeing Marcus and Francisco, they gave chase to them also.*

This is the opening description[1] of the racist incident against the 'Butetown Three' who were the subject of extreme racist abuse and violence by a number of white 'skinheads'. Bad enough in itself, but the response of the police following their initial reporting proved equally if not more damaging than the initial incident. We will use this case study to illustrate some of the important themes of this chapter.

Definitions of racist abuse and violence

This chapter will examine the meanings of racist abuse and violence for those experiencing it; the reasons why victims may be reluctant to report such incidents to the police and other agencies; and the overwhelming evidence that even when they do report, the likelihood of this resulting in prosecution of the perpetrators is extremely small. We explore ways in which this situation must and can change and how victims might be better helped, supported and empowered.

To begin, we need to examine what is generally understood by the terms 'racist abuse and violence'. 'From Murmur to Murder', the title of a training pack for probation officers working with racist offenders (Midlands Probation Training Consortium in Collaboration with Midlands Region Association of Chief Officers of Probation (ACOP) 1998) captures the full magnitude and scale of the problem. This is an issue that can pass unnoticed by the unaware white person when it is presented in 'subtle' language or veiled undertones (the 'murmur'). However, it can move from this through verbal offence and abuse to physical and psychological attack, bullying, harassment, injury and indeed murder, because of prejudice based on the difference in skin colour and/or ethnicity, between the victim and the perpetrator.[2]

The Association of Chief Police Officers (ACPO) in 1985 identified a common definition of the meaning of a 'racial incident':

> Any incident in which it appears to the reporting or investigating officer that the complaint involves an element of racial motivation; or any incident which includes an allegation of racial motivation made by any person. (ACPO Good Practice Guide for Police Response to Racial Incidents, cited in MPS submission to Part 1 of The Stephen Lawrence Inquiry, Macpherson 1999, p.205)

Lemos (2000) also identifies the distinguishing factors that turn abuse, vandalism or assault into racial harassment as being the motives of the perpetrator – racial hatred – and the impact on the victim – fear, distress and isolation. (Lemos 2000, p.4)

The ACPO definition was simplified by the Lawrence Inquiry to:

> a racist incident is any incident which is perceived to be racist by the victim or any other person. (Macpherson 1999, p.328)

This would suggest a positive, victim-led approach to the definition of racist abuse and violence. This also seems to be supported by the Crime and Disorder Act (1998) which created new offences of racially aggravated crime (Sections 28–32, and 82), including new assault, harassment and public order offences with significantly higher maximum penalties if it can be shown the offence was racially aggravated.

The following table suggests an increase in the reporting of racial crimes, with increased public awareness of the nature of racial abuse and violence.

Table 7.1 Reported racial incidents (Source: *Statistics on Race and Criminal Justice System,* Home Office 1998)	
1991	7,882
1992	7,734
1993/4	11,006
1994/5	11,878
1995/6	12,222
1996/7	13,151
1997/8	13,878

A 1997 Policy Studies Institute (PSI) Report, *Ethnic Minorities in Britain,* also measured the extent of what it termed 'low level' racial harassment. Respondents were asked whether they had been verbally abused or threatened. The PSI results suggest that in 1993/94 20,000 respondents were racially attacked, 40,000 were subjected to racially motivated property damage and 230,000 people were racially abused or insulted: that is, 290,000 people subjected to some form of racial harassment over a 12-month period, compared to the 143,000 reported by the British Crime Survey (cited in NACRO 2000).

However, findings from the 1998 British Crime Survey (BCS) on ethnic minorities' experience of crime show that fewer minority victims than white victims report racially motivated crime to the police: 29 per cent compared to 55 per cent of white victims (Home Office 1998). According to the BCS, 55 per cent of racist incidents were not reported, and this figure rises to 70 per cent when the victim was from an ethnic minority group (Lemos 2000).

> When reporting to the police victims may fail to mention evidence or perceptions of racism – even when racist allegations are made some incidents may not be recorded by the police, or at least not additionally recorded as racist incidents. (Percy 1998, cited in Lemos 2000, p.7)

Carson and Macleod (1997) explored the usage of concepts such as race and racism and other explanations of crime given by ethnic minority and white victims during interviews about victimisation experiences. They found that almost all the *offenders* involved in the crime incidents were white, yet relatively few ethnic minority *victims* said, when asked directly about crime causation, that they thought racism had been involved either in the target incident or in crime in general. The findings of their study suggest that perceiving race or racism to be a factor in crime victimisation may directly affect the distress felt by the victim, and partially explain the relatively greater suffering which may be experienced by ethnic minority persons. No wonder, then, if many black victims are reluctant to ascribe a racial motive to an attack or offence, which is distressing enough in itself without the added layer of racism as motivation. We ask the question: 'Are white professionals sufficiently alert to and aware of the potential reasons for this reluctance to ascribe a racial motivation?' Further, are they likely to ask the right questions and elicit the full picture from black victims? We speculate whether their own lack of knowledge and awareness, coupled with a lack of skills to deal with the resulting distress, contribute to the failure to identify the full scale of racially motivated crime.

Once victims summon up the courage to report a racist incident, what response might they expect from the criminal justice agencies? Bowling (1999) reminds us that according to official statistics in only about two per cent of all notifiable criminal offences is an offender caught and convicted. In the research undertaken in North Plaistow, in the London Borough of Newham, in the late 1980s and early 1990s, of those offences recorded by the police in the 18 months following the introduction of a new racial-incident policy aimed at increasing law enforcement, prosecution occurred in only 1.3 percent of cases: two out of 152 (Bowling 1999).

Marcus and Francisco reported the threats being made to them and Marcus's little sister Emma immediately:

Marcus and Francisco flagged down a police car and explained what was happening. The police officer advised them to get back in their car and follow him.

The police saw the skinheads and knew they had also spotted Marcus and Francisco. Another police vehicle was parked opposite. No-one intervened.

One skin then threw the bike at the car and another smashed the side window.

One skin was held by police as he continued to direct threats of violence and racist abuse. Marcus got out of the car whilst trying to defend himself against other skins; some were also attacking Francisco in the car. Marcus threw one punch and was then arrested by the police – who had been observing in the parked police vehicle. Francisco practically fell out of the car and tried to run away – shouting at the police "We're the victims, what do you think you are doing?"

He was then chased by police officers, CS sprayed in his face, and put in the back of an unventilated van.

The police and any on-lookers can surely have been in no doubt that this was a racist attack, and yet Marcus, the victim, was arrested for defending himself.

Bowling estimates that, calculated on the same basis as the Home Office statistics, about four racial incidents in 10,000 result in prosecution. One of the issues already mentioned appears to be failure to recognise the racial nature of the incident. In 1997 the Crown Prosecution Service (CPS) published the first results of its racial incidents monitoring scheme, which showed that of those cases identified by the CPS for prosecutions as racially motivated, only a third had been identified by the police – the remaining two-thirds were identified by CPS lawyers from information in the prosecution file (Midlands Probation Training Consortium 1998).

These figures suggest a massive under-reporting of the true extent of racially motivated crime, but also an alarming failure of the police both to record and successfully prosecute the perpetrators. According to NACRO (2000) the early indications from the 1998/99 monitoring are that police performance in identifying racial incident cases improved to the extent that they identified slightly over half of the cases submitted to the CPS for prosecution as racial incidents. However, given the general failure to record and prosecute racially motivated crime that these statistics indicate, is it any wonder that victims of such crime have little confidence in the authorities, and frequently do not report?

Other factors are also at play here. Fitzgerald (1994) discusses the ways in which crime is covered in the media depending on the race of the victim. He cites Los Angeles police chief Willie Williams as noting that stories about victims who are white, males, females, elderly females and foreigners, receive the most attention. Williams believed that more coverage of black murders could help to halt the violence. Certainly, a perusal of the British press would identify a preponderance of stories about black people as offenders rather than as victims. Ninety-nine per cent of Black people don't commit crimes and yet we see images of Black people day in and day out, and the impression they are all committing crime (Fitzgerald 1994, p.5).

Characteristics of the victims

About four per cent of black British people, five per cent of Indians and eight percent of Pakistanis and Bangladeshis experienced one or more racist crime during 1995 according to the British Crime Survey (1998). The Nottinghamshire Common Monitoring Scheme noted that of the victims of racially motivated crime in 1996/7, victims covered the full age span, with 11.4 per cent being under the age of 10, and that both genders experienced such crime almost equally. It, too, concluded that people of Pakistani origin are the most vulnerable to attack, followed by people of Indian origin and people of African-Caribbean origin (Midlands Probation Training Consortium 1998). These findings support our belief that racist attacks in Britain are experienced predominantly by black people.[3]

What is the experience of the victims of these attacks? Barnes and Ephross (1994) examined 'hate violence' in the United States, which they defined as criminal acts stemming from prejudice based on race, religion, sexual orientation, or ethnicity. The sample consisted of 59 victims and included black, white and southeast Asian people. More than half the victims reported experiencing a series of attacks rather than a single attack. Anger, fear and sadness were the emotional responses most frequently reported by victims. Lemos (2000) identifies as a distinguishing feature of racial harassment that the whole family is affected, including the children, even when not all family members have been attacked. He also suggests that being the victim of a racist attack increases the likelihood of conflict between spouses; children are escorted to school and denied the opportunity to play outside; relatives and friends are less likely to visit; the health of all members of the family deteriorates (Lemos 2000, p.8).

> *At the police station on the day, the two boys were interviewed without medical treatment, and with Marcus constantly asking about his sister. The police initially told him they had her, but then said things like 'What child?'.*
>
> *In fact, the Bahranian student had phoned the police after about an hour. Having being chased from the shop he had taken the girl to his home.*
>
> *When the police fetched Emma, they locked her in a waiting room with no social worker. When her mother arrived, she was not allowed in to her daughter until the arresting officer arrived.*
>
> *Emma's mother was not yet aware of the full story and nobody told her immediately – so she was faced with her daughter deeply distressed, telling her that a man had taken her to his house.*

There is also evidence to suggest that *fear* of crime is much greater amongst certain groups in society, including black and Asian groups,[4] and frequently is disproportionate to the actual risk of crime. For example, older people in general are much more fearful of personal attack and burglary than are younger people, although the actual likelihood of physical assault is highest for young men (Joseph 1997).

However, Joseph found from analysing a range of research data that elderly males experienced a higher rate of victimisation than elderly females and that black people *per se* were more likely than whites to be victims of crime,[5] although research on elderly black people is sparse. White (1982, cited in Joseph 1997), in his study on elderly blacks, found that fear of crime was an integral part of their daily lives. Because of their fear of crime, the elderly restricted their activities outside the home. Black males have the highest rate of victimisation of any group in the US and it is understandable, therefore, that black males might have a higher perception of vulnerability than black females.

The history of racist attacks

The history of racial attacks in Britain is well documented: Fryer (1984) and Chouhan and Jasper (2000) compile a twentieth-century chronicle of racial violence:

1919   Attacks on Arab seamen in South Shields, Cardiff and Liverpool.

1958   Attacks on ethnic minority communities in Nottingham, Camden Town, Kensington, and a large area of suburban London.

1961   Middlesbrough riot.

1981   Arson attack in Deptford.

1981   The Joint Committee against Racism presented the Home Office with a dossier of over 11,000 race attacks in 1981.

1981   A peak in racist murders (26 in this one year alone).

1991   Riots took place with elements of racial violence in their genesis.

1991   Murder of Rolan Adams.

1992   Murders of 10 ethnic minority people in London, Birmingham, Manchester and Newcastle.

1993   Murders of Ali Ibrahim Abu Zaid, Keith Harris, Stephen Lawrence and Fiaz Mirza.

1994   Murder of Mohan Singh Kullar.

1996   The white partners of three minority ethnic sports personalities threatened by letter bombs from European far right groups.

1997   After a racist attack Ricky Reel was found dead in the river Thames.

1998   Murder of Surjit Singh Chhokar.

2000   Murder of Zahid Mubarek by Robert Stewart, a man known by the prison authorities to be a violent racist, in the cell they shared at Feltham Young Offenders' Institution, five hours before Zahid's release from a 90-day sentence for theft and interfering with a motor vehicle.

The above is a shameful catalogue of the worst excesses of violent racism in Britain in the last 100 years. What is concealed behind these 'incidents' is the vast pool of trauma and distress caused to the many thousands of black people who are verbally and physically harassed and assaulted over, in some cases, many years. As Bowling highlights, one of the major problems in identification of such attacks and harassment is the manner in which they are identified, particularly by the police, as 'incidents' or 'one-offs', rather than identifying the 'act in context' (Bowling 1999, p.310). Bowling describes the notion of harassment as implying a series or sequence of events.

    Crawford and Goodey suggest that the message victimology and criminal justice practitioners should take from feminist and anti-racist research is the fact that:

> the continuum of lifetime experiences, relating to violence against women and ethnic minorities, is also shared by other significant sub-groups in the population who experience victimisation as an ongoing process throughout their lives. The interpretation of one incident of victimisation in isolation from a lifetime's experience of victimisation – as separate from that life-

time's experience of offending – may yield only limited understanding of the victimisation process. (Crawford and Goodey 2000, p.233)

What is being done to encourage victims to report?

In May 2000 the Home Office launched its Code of Practice on reporting and recording racist incidents (Home Office 2000) in response to recommendation 15 of the Stephen Lawrence Inquiry Report. As a result many local authorities and other agencies have instituted common reporting forms and third-party reporting centres. These include advice centres, places of worship and community centres. In a few areas, GP surgeries and public buildings such as libraries and schools have joined the reporting network.

Table 7.2 Measures to encourage reporting or share information (Lemos 2000: 20)		
	Areas (n=67)	*Percentage*
Third-party reporting centres	37	55
Common reporting form	39	58
Target to increase reporting	17	25

However, as Lemos identifies, while commendable, these measures are still patchy and the effectiveness of third-party reporting centres needs careful monitoring. In several local authorities training for staff in how to record incidents may have been provided, but it was not accompanied by enough training on how to deal with victims and what support to put into place immediately. We have also found examples where a school or community centre was a designated reporting centre, but the pupils or residents were unaware of this and/or did not know who to report to.

Using the case example as illustration, we chart the experiences of victims of racial abuse and violence and examine the likely response by people and agencies to the initial and subsequent reporting of the event.

Initial attack / fear of attack

Given the evidence of fear of crime highlighted earlier, before any form of attack or verbal abuse takes place we can assume that black people have a heightened awareness of their own vulnerability in relation to potential attacks. This, coupled with their knowledge of what has happened to other black people as victims, and the general sense of cynicism and fatalism with regard to the likely response of agencies to any attack, may predispose black people to feel a sense of 'victimisation' whether or not any attacks occur.[6]

Response by the public / others in the immediate vicinity

When attacks do occur it is hardly surprising if there is already doubt in the mind of the victim about the likely response from others around them:

> *Marcus and Francisco were now shouting for someone to get the girl out. A Bahranian student took the girl and shouted he would meet them later in the Spar shop.*

Another black person is the one to 'rescue' the child. However, he too then becomes a subject of the attack:

> *However, some skins had also gone to the shop and chased the student and Emma out and then seeing Marcus and Francisco, gave chase to them.*

Response by the police

> A great deal of creative endeavour is being expended on increased reporting. A similarly determined effort is needed to ensure that all racist incidents reports are accurately recorded. (Lemos 2000, p.7)

Since Scarman first identified the critical role of the police (Scarman 1981, p.210),

> Successive governments over the last twenty years have spent millions of pounds on race awareness training for police officers. Over the same period of time the police, particularly the Metropolitan Police, have developed equality policies in advance of other state agencies. In spite of this you are seven times more likely to be stopped by the police if you are Black than if

you are White; racists get away with murder; and Black officers still face racism from their colleagues. (Chouhan and Jasper 2000, p.5)

As identified by Bowling (1999) for both Scarman and the subsequent Macpherson report into the death of Stephen Lawrence, the central concern was related in some sense to a failure of policing. Macpherson concluded that the failure of the investigation was the result of 'professional incompetence, institutional racism and a failure of leadership by senior officers' (Macpherson 1999, p.317). Some examples of this are highlighted here:[7]

- Inspector Groves at the scene in 1993 did not recognise the possibility of a racial attack; they presumed a fight – the Inquiry took the view that this was an example of 'racist stereotypical behaviour.' (Macpherson 1999, p.322)

- The two Family Liaison officers (Detective Sergeant Bevan and Detective Constable Holden) who worked with the Lawrence family during the investigation did not conclusively accept that this was a racial attack even at the time of the inquiry in 1998. This is all the more remarkable as: The inquest verdict was that it had been an unprovoked racial attack; there had been a significantly increased number of racist attacks in the area in the last two years including the murders of Rohit Duggal and Rolan Adams; the BNP had been active in the area and in the time since they had set up a bookshop in Welling in 1989 racial attacks had increased 200% and there had been massive community campaigning including anti-BNP marches by the National Black Caucus. (Chouhan and Jasper 2000)

- The internal review (Barker) of the investigation was said to be flawed and indefensible by Macpherson. (Macpherson 1999, p.197)

- The surveillance team was not fully deployed immediately and as a result missed vital evidence, especially as they did not have the equipment to communicate what they saw. Incidentally the reason for the full team not being there was apparently that they had been sent to observe a young black man accused of petty theft from the person (Macpherson 1999, p.136). This is indicative of a policy

> decision which puts lower value on observing white murder
> suspects than it does on observing a young Black petty thief.
> (Chouhan and Jasper 2000)

Indeed there are many other examples from the Lawrence case, which high-light in particular the failure of intelligence-led policing with regard to racial attacks. This could signify a degree of indifference to the issue at the time. The appointment of John Grieve to head the Racial and Violent Crime Task Force (RV CTF – CO24) in August 1998 signaled a new, aggressive approach by the Metropolitan Police Service to racial attacks. John Grieve is noted for commenting that if the police can tackle terrorist attacks they must be able to do the same for racism.

> Within 18 months of the creation of the RV CTF there had been a 900%
> increase in racist/hate intelligence, and arrests and reporting increased by
> over 250%. (Grieve 2000, cited in Lemos 2000, p.13)

Similarly, the ACPO document on tackling hate crimes says:

> Our ultimate goal is eradication – this is no overnight task. A more tangible
> goal in many cases must be to reverse the positions in society of the victim
> and the offender. The offender often enjoys the comfort and anonymity of
> working from within the fabric of society against victims whose vulnerabil-
> ity may lie in their isolation from the mainstream...this at a strategic level, is
> a key component to providing protection and support for communities in
> relation to hate crime. They leave the hate motivated offender with a simple
> choice – change your behaviour if you want to be accepted. Break the law
> with hate crime and face society's censure and our positive arrest policy.
> (ACPO 2000, cited in Lemos 2000, p.9)

The Butetown Three might have wished that the police officers to whom they originally reported the initial incident had exercised this degree of clarity:

> *It was then discovered that CCTV had caught the whole incident. This clearly showed*
> *that it was a skinhead who had assaulted the police officer and that the police officers in*
> *the parked vehicle had watched the whole incident but had done nothing to intervene*
> *until they had moved to arrest Marcus and Francisco.*

In sum, the police failed them by failing:

- to recognise they were victims, not perpetrators
- to recognise that it was a racial attack
- to show due care and attention to their distress and medical needs at the police station
- to provide appropriate information and support to the mother and little girl.

The response of other agencies including Victim Support

On going to a solicitor for help, they were advised that as these were not huge charges, they should just plead guilty. Not satisfied with this, they tried the REC, the MP Alun Michael, local councillors and Emma's head teacher Betty Campbell who was the most helpful of them all. She in fact phoned the REC, but the REC did not or would not help. Several agencies failed them, including the REC, Victim Support (no communication) and local councillors.

They then went to the CAB where I (Hilary Brown) took the case on, and discharged the lawyers. I sought assistance from the Society of Black Lawyers and The 1990 Trust[8]

Victim Support is the national charity for victims of crime. All Victim Support services are governed by a national code of practice which aims to ensure that services are accessible to victims of crime from all communities. The code of practice also aims to ensure that nationally and locally the organisation is representative of the communities it serves (NACRO 2000).

Maguire and Kynch (2000) found that on the whole victims in categories reporting the highest levels of emotional impact and expressing the most need were more likely to be contacted by Victim Support schemes. These included victims of the more serious offences, poorer victims and those in 'exceptionally vulnerable' groups. However, exceptions were: victims from ethnic minorities, male victims of violence and victims of serial offences, threats and intimidations – all of which groups reported relatively high levels of impact and need, but relatively low contact rates with Victim Support. All of the above characteristics, as already identified, relate to victims of racist abuse and violence. Linked to this was the fact that awareness of Victim Support was fairly high across all sections of the population, but it was exceptionally low amongst the very elderly, black and Asian respondents – again, the groups most likely to be affected by fear of, and actual, racist abuse and violence. So not only is there a significantly lower contact by Victim Support to these groups, but there is a failure to transmit relevant information and knowledge to the groups who most need it.

NACRO identifies, however, that in all aspects of its services Victim Support is continuing to develop and monitor its responses to racist incidents and crimes. A service review was a major part of its strategic plan for 1999–2000. In response to the Stephen Lawrence Inquiry Report, the Government announced an increase in funding to Victim Support, so that its current £12.7m grant rose by 2001 to £19m (NACRO 2000, p.63).

Lemos identifies a team of 40 volunteers recruited by Victim Support in Tower Hamlets, eight of whom are currently able to take on racial harassment case work. Specialist training courses are held, for example on racial harassment and domestic violence (Lemos 2000, p.44).

The response of other criminal justice agencies: Crown Prosecution Service (CPS)/Courts/Probation

This was not recognised as a racist attack by senior police officers, nor the CPS who continued with the prosecution against Marcus and Francisco. At the Magistrates' Court it was adjourned twice – once because Shaun Kanavan did not turn up – although Marcus, who by now was studying in London, had travelled to Cardiff at his own expense. The judge was pressed to see the CCTV video footage.

At this, charges against Marcus and Francisco were dropped. They were given a Newton hearing to express their views on the attack, but they became victims of lawyers who wanted to show them in a bad light for the sake of the skinheads' defence. For two and a half hours, Marcus was questioned. The CPS never intervened to stop proceedings by questioning the relevance.

Another criminal justice service involved with victims of crime is the Probation Service which has a duty to operate a 'Victim Contact' scheme in which all victims of offenders receiving prison sentences of four years or more (recently reduced to 12 months) will be visited by a member of the Probation Service to ascertain their views and feelings on the release plans for the offender.[9] The Probation Service is also the main agency to tackle the perpetrators of racial crimes, and the training pack 'From Murmur to Murder', referred to earlier, provides a structured training programme for probation officers to use in this work.

Unfortunately, even where there is clear evidence of racist motivation, offenders are not necessarily referred to the Probation Service for intervention to address their racism. For example:

> *Eventually, three skins were given risible sentences: Shaun Kanavan (the one with the bike) was given a prison sentence of 12 months for criminal damage.*
>
> *John Sheppard, (associated with Combat 18[10]) was given a prison sentence of 6 months. (Interestingly his house was raided before the incident by police who had been aware that several fascists had arrived in Cardiff in 1997 when 50 years of the independence of India was to be celebrated.) However, the police had lost the evidence.*
>
> *Raymond Lovell, who assaulted the police officer, was given a community service order of 120 hours. He had many previous convictions.*

Identifying the particular needs of victims – considerations and recommendations

Primarily, the victims/survivors of racial harassment and attack want it to stop, and then they want to ensure justice. For all this they need support. The evidence so far shows that while confidence in reporting is increasing, confidence levels in clear-up or prosecution as a result are not justified. What kind of conditions are needed to make progress?

1. Awareness of the reality of racism

Any people or agencies responding to a racial 'incident' should arrive at the scene with an awareness of the reality of racism, and an acknowledgement, if not of the detail, at least of the context, in which such racial incidents occur in British society.

> It is the Trust's view that our institutions are informed by a predominantly white British culture. Embedded in that culture is the history and politics of a nation which murdered, enslaved, colonised and still legislates against Black people. This underpins a pervasive culture of white superiority, racist thinking and behaviour. It is this culture and its impact on the custom and practice of an organisation which can result in widescale discrimination both within service delivery and employment practices, whether the organisation does or does not have overtly discriminatory policies. (Chouhan and Jasper 2000, p.3)

It is therefore necessary to ensure:

2. Education and training

Many organisations have trained their staff in awareness about equal opportunities. However, specific knowledge and skills are needed for dealing effectively with racist abuse and violence. Lemos suggests that these relate in the first instance to recognising the problem when presented with it, especially if the victim or person reporting the incident does not describe it, or perhaps even recognise it as racially motivated (Lemos 2000, p.16). In addition, knowing how to record accurately and consistently and being able to trigger immediate support and help from a range of agencies is critical.

3. Agencies involved in responding to an incident take a collaborative and multi-agency action approach

The criticisms levelled at the police during the 1980s that they were not accountable to the local community with regard to racial incidents, were intended to be resolved by a multi-agency approach (Bowling 1999). The Newham project suggests that to a large extent the 'conflict between agencies was mediated by the existence of the multi-agency approach' (Bowling 1999, p.298). Multi-agency working has long been promoted.

The House of Commons Home Affairs Select Committee recommended in 1986:

> All police forces and local authorities whose areas contain an appreciable ethnic minority population should give serious consideration to the establishment of a multi-agency approach to racial incidents. (Cited in Lemos 2000, p.10)

With the Crime and Disorder Act (1998) multi-agency forums have become part of a wider crime and disorder strategy. Unfortunately Bowling concludes that the multi-agency approach did not really bring about an improvement in the effectiveness of action against racial incidents. He believes, for example, that residents in North Plaistow are not really any safer on the streets or in their beds as a result of the introduction of the new approach. He concludes that while the approach has resulted in making the police more aware of the problem, there is no evidence to suggest that it has affected, or indeed could affect, the police decision to take action in individual instances of violent racism, or the decision to take action in general (Bowling 1999).

One of the clearest examples of multi-agency failure is exemplified by the case study. However the case of Mal Hussain and Linda Livingstone is also illustrative of a catalogue of multi-agency failure.[11] Since 1991 Mal Hussain and Linda Livingstone, who own a small grocery store on the Ryelands estate in Lancaster, have suffered a phenomenal 2000+ racial attacks. These include two shooting incidents, stonings, six firebomb attacks, and death threats. So far there have been 50 successful prosecutions but the harassment continues. The city council has recently defended itself successfully against Mal Hussain's claim that they should have taken action against the perpetrators, on the grounds that Mal Hussain is not one of their tenants. This cuts right across the duty that local authorities have under the Race Relations Act 1976[12] to promote good race relations and ensure equality of opportunity. The police, for their part, seem powerless to deal with the perpetrators, even though the attacks are said to be orchestrated by a core of five families on the estate.

The 1990 Trust has created a scheme called 'Share in Anti-Racism', whereby people can donate money to the Mal Hussain case, for which they are deemed to be buying a share in anti-racism. With the money raised the aim is to buy Mal Hussain and Linda Livingstone out of the property and help them into a new life elsewhere. This innovative scheme is of course a good idea, but it should not be that Mal Hussain's case is left to a charity and the good will of some of the public. This is a societal responsibility, and if such creativity can emerge from the voluntary sector it can and must be matched at least by the authorities. Now is not the time to be defending reputations and elected members. If only the same amount of energy and money that authorities spend on defending their positions were invested in helping the real victims here, the problem might well have been solved by now.

4. When racist incidents are reported they are acted upon by the police and wherever possible prosecution follows

The Home Secretary has set a performance indicator for police on 'the percentage of reported racist incidents where further investigative action is taken and the percentage of racially aggravated crimes detected' (Lemos 2000, p.12). As reporting and recording increase, so too will the confidence of victims in the system's ability to respond. It will be important to monitor the results of the Racial and Violent Crimes Task Force headed up by John Grieve.

5. Victims of racial abuse and attack might also wish, as identified by Bowling (1999), that there could be a shift of focus towards the offenders who perpetrate the attacks

This is not to deny the importance of identifying the perceptions and experiences of victims, but the real and ultimate solution to the problem lies in tackling the motivation of the perpetrators. 'From Murmur to Murder', the training pack for probation officers working with racially motivated offenders, is a very important contribution to this area of work.

HM Inspectorate of Probation, in its thematic report *Towards Race Equality* (2000), identifies research undertaken by the Home Office in 1997 which indicated that there was a need for a cultural shift within the Probation Service if the service was to work effectively with racially motivated and racist offenders.

> ...the very culture of the Probation Service, with its strong commitment to equal opportunities and its disapproving stance on racist behaviour, appeared to mitigate against offenders ever admitting to this aspect of their offending...offenders' racist attitudes – which were perceived to be common and reflecting normal local attitudes – remain hidden. To some extent it appeared that the probation officers welcomed this since, if an offender did display racist attitudes, they would not know what to do about it other than invoke the local disciplinary procedures for failing to respect the service's equal opportunities policy.[13] (Home Office 2000)

The HM Inspectorate report recommends that probation committees and chief probation officers should adopt the definition of a racist incident in the Macpherson report and produce revised policy and practice guidelines to ensure the effective supervision of racially motivated offenders.

6. A range of security measures for victims

For example:

- CCTV
- English language courses
- panic button telephone units
- phone helplines
- Ringmaster (computer controlled telephone dialing recorded message system used to pass information to watch schemes from potential victims of crime)
- anti-arson attack measures – mailboxes, fire extinguishers, smoke and flame detectors (ACPO 2000).

7. Support for victims

We would also concur with the proposals from the Lemos and Crane research (Lemos 2000) where they call specifically for a national racial attacks hotline. This is in view of the fact that victims often talk about the need to have one number on which they can have confidence in action. This hotline should have regularly updated information from all available agencies (police, racial attacks projects, victim support, housing authorities, etc.) in the different areas of Britain, accessible by a database. 24-hour lines are available in some areas, as shown above. This should also assist in recording numbers of racial incidents and encouraging those people who 'only' experience 'verbals' at least to report it. This, as Lemos points out, is extremely valuable information for gathering intelligence on the whereabouts and profiles of perpetrators.

However, we would also suggest that local action is vital for capacity building in a community. Over-reliance on a nationalised service should not be the only way to empower communities.

It is therefore critical to support the black voluntary sector, especially organisations concerned with supporting victims and monitoring responses by the authorities. It is somewhat ironic that up and down the country racial attacks monitoring projects have suffered massive budget cuts in the last decade and some have had to shut down completely, yet these were the very organisations with the best potential to support black communities. In some instances in the Newham monitoring project, staff were known to arrive at incidents faster than, or at the same time as, the police (Bowling 2000). Local people who know the areas well are often best placed to respond appropriately in supporting victims, and also know which individuals in the local authorities are likely to act.

We also await the results of the Victim Support review and the need to address appropriate support for black victims.

Conclusion

If a person or family does not feel safe and secure in their home environment or on the streets because of the colour of their skin, this debilitates their capacity for civic engagement and social inclusion. Is it any wonder that in areas of underachievement and exclusion of Bangladeshi or African/Caribbean young people in schools, there is evidence of high levels of racial attack? A young boy of 12 recently spoke to us about the need to spend the first year at secondary school ensuring his safety throughout the rest of his school experience. He has had to make strategic relationships; be involved in and win fights; deal with the dilemma of reporting, and being labelled and further victimised as a 'grass'; know which routes to go home by and which to avoid, and so on. No wonder his mind cannot be fully on his studies; he is lucky in that he goes to a school where there are plenty of black children in a predominantly black area.

A large part of the solution to exclusion and underachievement is to be able to ensure the safety of these children. How can we ask them to take full part in the mainstream of society and eventually sit on this or that board or quango or be involved in the democratic system if they live to survive? They have not the luxury of lifestyle choice. Of course poverty is also a major factor, and it goes hand in hand with increased levels of racial attacks.

Surely it should not have been the responsibility of voluntary organisations to provide the best support to the Butetown Three? It has been a similar story with regard to the plight of Mal Hussain and Linda Livingstone. It must be possible for the agencies in Lancaster to do something to move them out while they are still alive, and tackle the the perpetrators of the harassment. It will not be long before the strengthened Race Relations Act and Human Rights Act are invoked in this case. What will the authorities do then?

To achieve a level of justice for victims it is necessary to have not just policy-framed anti-racist police services, Crown Prosecution Services, etc., but also:

- personnel who know the conditions that lead to racist attacks and therefore use preventative measures as well

- anti-racist training and specific training in dealing with racial attacks, to include: knowing and using the new definition, knowing how to record accurately and consistently, and being able to trigger immediate support and help from a range of agencies

- a criminal justice system which sentences heavily and consistently to demonstrate that racial attack is a serious crime and not a matter of opinion

- support for the victims from voluntary and statutory agencies, with trained and well resourced workers.

This is the responsibility not just of the police and CPS, but also of the criminal justice system in general, as well as of housing agencies, youth services, social services, education establishments, voluntary agencies and others.

Notes

1. Information provided by Hilary Brown, who was at the time from Cardiff Citizens' Advice Bureau, and has worked to support and help the 'Butetown Three'. These extracts are quoted with the permission of the 'Butetown Three'.

2. We believe that most racism in this country is experienced by people of a different skin colour from the majority white population. However, we recognise that racist abuse and violence can also be directed at people from a wide range of ethnic minorities.

3. Black is used here as a political concept encompassing all people with a skin colour other than 'white' in a generic group that generally shares an ethnic origin influenced by a colonial past (Midlands Probation Training Consortium 1998).

4. Maguire and Kynch (2000) in their report based on data from the 1998 British Crime Survey).

5. Joseph cites: Bureau of Justice Statistics in the USA in 1983, 1991, 1992; Cook, Skogan and Antunes 1978; Ennis 1967; Reiss 1967.

6. Carson and Macleod (1997) suggest that on learning of the victimisation of members of one's own group, feelings of fear may be enhanced (they cite Skogan and Maxfield 1981; Tyler 1984), and that more specifically ethnic minority persons may feel an increased vulnerability to crime (Riger and Gordon 1981).

7. These observations arise from work undertaken by Karen Chouhan in the production of *A Culture of Denial: A Report by the 1990 Trust on the Stephen Lawrence Inquiry* (2000). Karen attended the majority of the inquiry hearings.

8. The 1990 Trust is a national black organisation set up out of the National Black Caucus as an information and policy unit and a registered charity. The organisation aims to promote good race relations, engage in policy development and articulate the needs of black communities from a grass roots perspective.

9. The Victim's Charter created an obligation for the Probation Service to contact victims (and the victims' families) of life sentence prisoners, prior to any consideration of an offender's release, to enquire whether they have any anxieties about the offender's release. (Home Office 1990, para.21)

10. A right-wing fascist organisation.

11. Information cited with the permission of Mal Hussain, who is known to Karen Chouhan.

12. Strengthened in 2001 by the Race Relations (Amendment) Act to include nearly all public sector organisations, and will now require more stringent monitoring.
13. Home Office: *The Perpetrators of Racial Harassment and Racial Violence.* Research Study 176 (1997), cited in *Towards Race Equality*, HM Inspectorate Thematic Inspection Report 2000, p.77.

References

Association of Chief Police Officers (2000) *Identifying and Combating Hate Crime.* ACPO.

Barnes A. and Ephross P. H. (1994) 'The impact of hate violence on victims; Emotional and behavioural responses to attacks.' *Social Work* 39, 3, May.

Bowling B. (1999) *Violent Racism: Victimisation, Policing and Social Context.* Oxford: Oxford University Press.

Carson L. and Macleod M. D. (1997) 'Explanations about crime and psychological distress in ethnic minority and white victims of crime: A qualitative exploration.' *Journal of Community and Applied Social Psychology* 7, 361–375.

Chouhan K. and Jasper L. (2000) *A Culture of Denial: A Report by the 1990 Trust on the Stephen Lawrence Inquiry.* London: 1990 Trust.

Crawford A. and Goodey J. (2000) *Integrating a Victim Perspective within Criminal Justice.* Dartmouth: Ashgate.

Fitzgerald M. (1994) 'Covering crime in black and white (racial aspects of press coverage of crime).' *Editor and Publisher 127*, 37, p.12.

Fryer P. (1984) *Staying Power: The History of Black People in Britain.* London and Sydney: Pluto Press.

Grieve J. (2000) *Institutional Racism: Does it Exist in the Police Service?* www.met.police.uk

Home Office (1990) *The Victims' Charter: A Statement of the Rights of Victims of Crime.* London: Home Office.

Home Office (1998) *Section 95 Statistics on Race and the Criminal Justice System.* Research, Development and Statistics Directorate. London: Home Office.

Home Office (1998) *Crime and Disorder Act 1998.* London: Stationery Office.

Home Office (1999) *Section 95 Statistics on Race and the Criminal Justice System.* London: Home Office.

Home Office (2000) HM Inspectorate of Probation: *Thematic Inspection Report – Towards Race Equality.* London: Home Office.

Joseph, J. (1997) Fear of crime among Black elderly. *Journal of Black Studies, 27*, 5 698–718.

Lemos G. (2000) *Racial Harassment: Action on the Ground.* Lemos and Crane, 20 Pond Square, London, N6 6LR.

Macpherson W. (1999) (advised by Tom Cook, The Right Reverend Dr John Sentamu and Dr Richard Stone) *The Stephen Lawrence Inquiry.* Cm 2462–1. London: Stationery Office.

Maguire M. and Kynch J. (2000) *Public Perceptions and Victims' Experiences of Victim Support. Findings from the 1998 British Crime Survey.* Research, Development and Statistics Directorate. London: Home Office.

Midlands Probation Training Consortium in Collaboration with Midlands Region ACOP (1998) *From 'Murmur to Murder': Working with Racist Offenders.* Birmingham: MPTC.

NACRO (2000) *Let's Get it Right. Race and Justice 2000.* NACRO Race Issues Advisory Committee. London: NACRO.

Percy A. (1998) *Ethnicity and Victimisation: Findings from the 1996 British Crime Survey.* London: Home Office.

Scarman, Lord (1982) *The Scarman Report: Report of an Inquiry into the Brixton Disorders* 10–12 April 1981. Cm London: HMSO.

8.

Probation Work
with Victims of Crime

Barbara Tudor

Reparation in the probation context

At the outset I will define the term 'reparation' for the purposes of what follows here; I am going to take a wide-ranging definition in order fully to explore some of the issues in which I think reparative work has an enormous and seriously under-researched contribution to make to so many of the concepts that are currently spoken of in political and criminal justice fields.

'Reparation' means 'any kind of repair'. The first time that this concept was formally introduced into probation work was in 1985 when the Home Office invited offers of interest for four pilot studies to look into the question of reparation in criminal justice systems. People working in these pilots found themselves engaging in a mediative process between victims and offenders in order to explore the possibilities for repair of the damage caused by offences. Some re-named their schemes, preferring the title 'mediation', as they felt that this properly valued the work being undertaken. There is no doubt that the *process* of victim–offender engagement itself is often the repair that is required, particularly in the case of very serious offences, where the possibility of repayment or repair in financial or work terms is clearly inappropriate. The questions that some victims need to have answered in order to fill in the gaps in their own knowledge, be empowered to make their own judgements and decisions, and thereby move on, can only be asked of offenders.

In some cases neither victims nor offenders will have any chance of rehabilitation into their former positions until they have been able to work through some constructive exchange of information or viewpoints in order to understand their own and others' situations better. Some serious offences with very sinister implications arise from long-standing, bitter disputes where views have become too entrenched for any acknowledgement of the other parties concerned, particularly often the victims.

Recently the term 'restorative justice' has become widely used, particularly since the Thames Valley Police began conferencing in Aylesbury. For some this term has become the new, overarching description which embraces all interventions of a reparative kind, while others use it in a very narrow context to describe a type of conferencing including victims and offenders and representation from their communities.

Despite the varied appropriations of the term, it could be argued that the use of the word 'justice' here is potentially misleading. For what is currently happening is that some legislation and guidance is attempting to 'ride two horses'. While continuing to base the system itself in a deeply adversarial context, terminology is beginning to develop which suggests that workers should adopt 'restorative principles' in pursuing their interactions with young offenders. This seems to indicate that we may be in a period of change in the culture of our criminal justice system, but certainly the way in which terminology is being used indicates a degree of confusion which encourages researchers and other professionals to engage in semantic arguments, not always to the benefit of service deliverers, or indeed those who may wish to receive service.

Within this climate and born of other difficulties surrounding the use of the word 'mediation' which in the middle 1990s was often understood to require that victims and offenders *must* meet face to face, West Midlands Probation Service began to use the term 'victim–offender' work, the hope being that this would indicate any area of work where victims and offenders would be consulted and engaged for a reparative or restorative purpose, especially that of making some amends for the damage caused either practically, financially or emotionally. This may be achieved through an indirect or direct process, one-to-one, or on a larger scale (conferencing of various types, and so on) if appropriate.

There are some specific and set models for these interactions, such as victim–offender mediation, restorative conferencing, family group conferencing, but there are very many interventions in between, which suit the people who engage in the process. Some involve work solely in individual cases with either victims or offenders. It is the aim of this work which is important. It must always be undertaken with the other party(ies) in mind. Hence victim contact work, victim perspective work with offenders in the course of report writing, in supervision, in group work, in custody and on release into the community, may be carried out within the parameters of restorative principles. This means that face-to-face or indirect communication of any type between victim and offender is always available and can be facilitated in any case, at any point, if it is appropriate and required to meet the needs of the victim and the offender.

This not only indicates a very substantial and far-reaching change for probation service staff, it also requires many similar changes in the working of all related systems and services. Should our system really begin to develop in this way, it might be appropriate to speak of 'restorative justice'. Currently we are on the very remote fringes of such a possibility.

Probation service workers strive to rehabilitate offenders with whom they are working positively into their communities. In order to rehabilitate victims too, repair of the damage they have caused in offending forms a core part of this work.

As long as work continues with offenders in isolation, without contact being made with victims, offenders will be denied the opportunity to make amends for their behaviour, and workers will collude with their lack of knowledge and understanding of the direct effects of their offending behaviour. Working with offenders and victims on the basis of assumptions gained from the conclusions of wide-scale studies of victimisation will fail to be effective on an individual basis. In individual cases practice will be too distant from reality.

Historical background

In the past the Probation Service's notion of reparation for offending behaviour has been invested in community service, i.e., sentencers made disposals requiring that offenders make reparation for their behaviour by undertaking a specific number of hours working for beneficiaries in the community. This work has rarely been organised in a way that makes it directly available to the actual victim of any specific offender. Indeed, on the whole, victims would never be informed that an offender had been sentenced to undertake community service, let alone be asked if anything could be undertaken to offer them personal repair, or if they would particularly wish an offender to do anything in the community that would be of relevance to themselves. Occasionally offenders have been supervised in fitting new locks, effecting repairs or decorating for personal victims, but there has always been a reticence on the part both of victim organisations and of probation services to engage in this type of work to any great extent. In many ways those undertaking community service have almost been encouraged not to think of their personal victims but to regard themselves as having repaid their debt to 'society'.

It could be argued that the whole of the system tends to reflect this rather distant means of dealing with offences as far as victims are concerned. It would appear that, as those involved in sentencing and working with offenders attempted to think out more effective ways of punishing offenders and engaged in discussions about the merits of custodial as opposed to community sentences, thinking became very much isolated from the feelings, needs and problems of direct victims. Against this background a victims' lobby began to emerge and has grown stronger and more cohesive over the last 30 years or so.

Recently there have been many comments about the development of victim perspectives within the probation service, as though this had 'just appeared'. Of course such developments do not just happen. The Probation Service has long been involved in working with victims, but until the publication of the first Victim's Charter this work tended to be more 'at arm's length'. Involvement in the development of a more realistic victim perspective throughout the criminal justice system has been taking place in this country since the late 1960s, when inter-agency groups began to discuss and explore the impact of crime on victims. This led to the development of victim support schemes in many local areas, strongly encouraged and supported by probation services. Constitutionally, Victim Support boards of trustees mandatorily include a non-voting representative of the local probation service or social services department. Most regard a probation service representative as an essential member of the committee, even though probation officers are no longer able to take up executive positions.

Throughout the 1970s developments continued, particularly in the areas of rape, domestic violence and child abuse.

The 1984 Probation Rules introduced the requirement that

> it shall be part of the duties of a probation officer to participate in such arrangements concerned with the prevention of crime or with the relationship between offenders and their victims or the community at large as may be approved by the Probation Committee on the advice of the Chief Probation Officer. [Rule 37]

This encouraged an interest in some of the new developments encompassed by the four reparation pilot schemes partially funded by the Home Office in 1985/1986. Three of the four units established in Cumbria, Leeds, Wolverhampton and Coventry were funded through probation services and staffed by them (Marshall and Merry 1990). Today three still exist, integrated into West Yorkshire and West Midlands Probation Services. A number of other services have made partnership arrangements to provide the opportunity for communication (usually mediation, occasionally also practical reparation) between victims and offenders, and some have experimented with in-service provision. It is not surprising that the early schemes did survive in probation services as this work is particularly relevant to the service primarily concerned with challenging offending behaviour and encouraging accountability. However, resource issues have prevented much potential progress hitherto.

Recent developments

In 1990 the Victim's Charter (Home Office 1990) introduced the requirement for probation services to make contact with victims of offenders given life sentences to inform them of the sentence and release from custody and give them the opportunity to express their anxieties or concerns regarding certain aspects of release which might be taken into consideration by decision-makers. This duty was taken up slowly, but brought much more into the development of probation services' work with victims after the publication of national standards for work with offenders, (HO 1995) which placed the duty on probation services to contact all victims of serious sexual and violent offences which have occasioned a custodial sentence of four years and over.

In West Midlands probation area, where two of the original reparation pilots were established, this duty was positively welcomed and widened to include all victims of such offences by offenders sentenced to custody of one year or over. This recognises the level of trauma that victims are likely to have experienced, and enables victims to take advantage of the reparative opportunity to be notified of the sentence within two months – to help them recover from some of the effects of the offence and begin planning their futures in the knowledge that they will have an opportunity to express their views at planning for release, which could assist in the assessment and management of actual or perceived risk. Within the service policy there is also the facility to offer contact to victims who do not fit into the above category if it is felt that it would be of particular benefit for them.

In order to assist with this wide-ranging development, the Association of Chief Officers of Probation (ACOP) and national Victim Support issued a joint statement in July 1996 (ACOP/VS 1996). Also in 1996, the Victim's

Charter was updated and reprinted (Home Office 1996), introducing the piloting of one-stop shops and victim statements. The production of victim personal statements commences in October 2001, with guidance expected in the summer. The statements will be available to all agencies working within the system, if the victim decides to make one. Although factual and carefully structured within a legal framework, sadly the statements will not necessarily contain information useful in terms of restoration as such, but they could assist in the preparation of pre-sentence and other reports, and in preparations by staff for victim contact or enquiries.

In 1998/9 new provisions were built into the youth justice legislation, making very considerable demands throughout the system with regard to victim contacts and the offer of restorative work. The introduction of new orders, such as reparation orders, action plan orders and anti-social behaviour orders, demands consideration of the victim perspective in some depth, but also written into the legislation was the requirement for a clearly discernible reparation aspect to be incorporated in all orders, including detention and training orders. This represents an enormous culture change in the way in which professionals work with young offenders, and currently it is evident that this work is in its infancy. Very experienced members of West Midlands Probation Service victim–offender work staff have been working with the pilot team in Wolverhampton since its inception in 1998, introducing victim reparative work. The scale of the new legislative demands is just becoming evident. It is already clear that some probation service and social services staff will find their social work skills invaluable in engaging with this agenda, but need to widen their thinking and training to encompass victim work.

In 1999 HM Inspectorate of Probation undertook a thematic inspection into victim work in probation services. The report was published in early 2000 as *The Victim Perspective: Ensuring the Victim Matters* (HMIP 2000). The inspection acknowledged a wide diversity in the way in which services had implemented the requirements of the Victim's Charter (Home Office 1990), national standards and Probation Circular 61/96. It also acknowledged that the circular had by no means taken into account the complexity and range of work with victims with which the probation service would have to engage. In his foreword HM Chief Inspector of Probation paid tribute to the finding that 'the Service has taken a constructive approach to implementing the contact service to victims, placing their concerns and safety first' and acknowledges that the work 'is demanding and requires a high level of skill in balancing both the rights of the victim and the rights of the offender'.

Sir Graham Smith further comments: '... delivering this service has involved a fundamental shift towards the perspective of the victim' (*ibid*). The report itself stated that it was too early to establish which model of delivering this work was best – and due to the circular's rather vague parameters a great variety of means of meeting its requirements have developed. The report also acknowledged that no resources had been directly allocated for this work. The inspection led to the preparation of Circular 108/00, effective as from April 2001, under which victim contact work becomes statutory. Prepared in consultation with a wide range of representatives from the field and various Home Office departments, the circular requires victim contact to be extended to all victims of serious violent and sexual offenders who have been sentenced to one year or more in custody.

> The Inspection acknowledged that...a number of services have developed a range of schemes for victims which are of a restorative nature. Such schemes can enhance a sense of justice for victims, reduce the fear of crime and also through more effective supervision of offenders, reduce the risk of re-offending. [foreword]

Because of resource difficulties the provision of such opportunities remains discretionary for services, although there can be little doubt that the increased work within victim contact and the development of staff skills in this area will bring much more heavy demand for victim–offender and restorative work in general.

In some probation areas (West Midlands is one of them) the development of victim contact work led to a lack of concentration on victim–offender work – national standard work being considered to be of higher priority, and new staff being supported by experienced members who had been undertaking victim–offender work for a number of years. Sometimes it can feel as though victim contact is only 'half the job', a feeling expressed by a number of restorative/reparative facilitators. It remains to be seen how far the development of the victim contact task will move into the wider restorative sector.

Possibly during the next few years an unrelenting process will take place towards more widely based restorative work in the probation service. The skills required to undertake this sensitive and highly complex work derive from social work and counselling, but they will need to be made available to a much wider range of professional and voluntary workers than in the past. Dealing with the tension of working between victims and offenders is challenging and demanding and requires training, prior thought and strong support from management. The integration of victim-related work is likely to be a growth area within the new National Probation Service in the beginning twenty-first century.

Other developments in the field of victim perspectives are under way. As the Probation Thematic Inspection proposals are implemented, and the new demands of Circular 108/2000 are introduced at the same time as the inception of the new National Probation Service, referral orders will be introduced as the first disposal for most young people who plead guilty to offences that are unlikely to result in custody on their first appearance in court. Such young people will be referred to a youth offender panel consisting of two trained community volunteers and a Youth Offending Team advisor. The panel will involve the offenders, their families and other people who are significant to them. Victims will also be invited to attend. If they do not wish to attend in person they may make the panel aware of their views by means of a statement or through a representative.

The future of reparative work in probation

The beginning of April 2001 saw a whole raft of new services which take new, much more wide-ranging cognisance of the victim's perspective and needs within the whole criminal justice system. However, there are some marked deficits in this provision and also some major resource implications and technical difficulties which are yet to be resolved. The implementation of these new dimensions of work will make heavy demands for training and support. Managers' understanding and commitment will be crucial in developing new structures for the proper representations of victims' needs and views. Information services, such as victim contact work and more intricate services providing facilitated interaction with offenders, are relatively short-term and sometimes sporadic interventions. However, they often uncover the need for support or access to other services, such as police, prisons, criminal injuries compensation and counselling, health and social services. We can expect further demands in all these areas, and of course there will be a need for inter-agency liaison to develop lines of communication and determine boundaries and responsibilities. This increased activity fits well into crime reduction and community safety strategies, as well as many of the inter-agency provisions, such as public protection panels and sex offender registers, which have recently been highlighted and developed due to strong victim demands, amplified by the media. This is another example of work requiring joint action from probation, prison and police personnel to further victims' safety.

Although there is a plethora of new proposals there are also some substantial gaps to note. There has been rapid development, but this still represents patchy provision, and different forms of discrimination exist concerning victims. The new youth justice legislation demands that when young people commit offences, victims should be contacted to obtain their views about reparation which would assist themselves or others. In the event of their having no specific individual views, they can expect to be informed of the likely reparative activity undertaken by the young person. Many of the victims of young people sentenced to detention and training orders are to be contacted under the requirements of Youth Justice Board National Standards (YJB 2000) and Probation Circular 108/2000. These may overlap in some cases, according to the age of the offender at and during sentence. The Youth Justice Board expects that by April 2003 effective restorative procedures will be in operation in 80 per cent of Youth Offending Teams, and that by 2004

80 per cent of interventions with offenders will have a victim component (Youth Justice Board 2001).

It is expected that contact provisions will be expanded to offer broader parity in the treatment of victims of mentally disordered offenders and other offenders under a new Mental Health Act. This means that victims will have to be contacted within two months of sentence and be invited to receive further information at key points in sentence, for example the preparation for parole reports, town leaves, release, and so on, when they may wish to provide information to decision-makers – as a result of which supervising probation officers or medical officers may request specific conditions in licences, and indeed supply information to groups such as public protection panels, to enable them to make more realistic risk assessments and plan risk management. It is more than likely that these services will lead to greater demand for, and take-up of, restorative victim–offender activities – but what about those victims who do not fit these criteria?

For many years practitioners working in the field of reparation in this broad sense have been well aware that the effects of offences upon victims are as varied and individual as the reasons for offenders committing offences. Some of the most difficult offences for victims to recover from are domestic burglaries, assaults, robberies, and what sometimes seem like minor car thefts. For some victims re-victimisation is also a major feature in these offences. Many are young people, particularly often young males, victims of street assaults and muggings. Support services are very thin for this particular group, which is often very badly affected and may particularly need access to information from or about offenders in order to assist their return to a more secure, normal life pattern. Those who regularly work with sexual and violent offenders are very aware that they are frequently scarred by similar victimisation in the past, and that this has been a major cause of their offend-ing, yet there is still a paucity of services for dealing with such victimisation. Many such victims fall outside of any category for whom victim contact or victim–offender services are available. The system itself currently operates in an openly discriminatory way.

For all the new legislation and provision outlined above, the current resource problems in providing for this work will not be easily overcome. While probation boards will have a little more funding to cover extended contact work in their own local areas, other services for victims will be provided at their discretion. For the vast majority of areas in the new service, the circular demands a huge extension of work, some of which is only just begun.

Also, the ability actually to make contact with victims depends primarily on being able to locate them. Current data protection law and human rights legislation can be problematic. Appropriate information needs to be made accessible to criminal justice workers who are mandated to do the work. Training and accreditation provisions, although under way, are not yet in place, and there are substantial gaps in the knowledge and understanding of many service personnel, both practitioners and managers, particularly at senior level. Rapid change has taken place in other areas of service intervention and youth justice legislation, and the set time-frames are a real constraint.

The role of research

It seems that research is often undertaken at the outset of new interventions when it can offer useful insights and recommendations. Good examples of this are early research conducted in 1985–1987 by Marshall and Merry (1990) and the interim report produced by James Dignan and published as an occasional paper by the Home Office in February 2000 (Dignan 2000). Such documents can be of immense value if issued quickly enough. The publication of *Crime and Accountability* (Marshall and Merry 1990), a wide-ranging document, was so badly delayed that a great deal of its usefulness was lost and many people drew their own conclusions about the political climate in the light of its non-availability.

James Dignan's *Interim Report on Reparative Work and Youth Offending Teams* (Dignan 2000) read like the answer to a prayer for a few long-term, committed restorative workers who had clung on to the practice because of the very clearly visible benefits to those victims and offenders with whom they worked. The report spoke clearly of the incipient culture change required to incorporate genuine reparation. However, the last tranche of the research is still unpublished at the time of writing, despite the fact that Youth Offending Teams came into existence and practice in April 2000. The piloting period was very brief for such a large venture, and the consolidated research not available in time to inform early developments nationally.

Frequently, following early development, substantial work begins to take place in the new area, informed by developing practice. It is to be hoped that this leads to stable periods of provision and to awareness of how far the procedures engaged in are applicable. In the case of the Coventry Reparation Unit this led to engagement in all aspects of probation service work, through all activities from Youth Liaison Panel and caution, through all courts, including civil and licencing courts, and into custodial institutions. Work between victims and offenders was available through all orders and there was a victim component in every groupwork intervention. Some work was undertaken within the Racial Harassment Forum and with neighbourhood disputes which came to inter-agency notice.

During this time no national researchers took any interest whatsoever, despite many approaches being made. Local research undertaken for annual reports within the Race Equality Council or the unit itself, including small scale findings from crown court intervention, were regarded as unscientific, unrepresentative or naïve. An official once commented, after reading of the reduction in custodial sentences, and successful rehabilitation of a dozen offenders who had taken part in the first year of operation in the crown court: 'Not a penny is saved until an institution closes'. The life experiences of victims and offenders were clearly irrelevant in this thinking, and therefore easily written off.

Researchers frequently took no account of participants' needs or wishes. Quantitative measures such as recidivism and financial or material repayment were used instead of qualitative measures of participant satisfaction. Concentration on only one aspect, particularly recidivism, can further emphasise the focus on offenders and encourage inappropriate approaches to victims.

Implications for future research

There are many areas of probation service work with victims that warrant long-term, in-depth research. There is a real need to look into the actual processes in which practitioners engage and to measure the satisfaction of all concerned. Alongside this there is a need for some before-and-after research into participants' expectations and what psychological changes have occurred throughout the entire process – many practitioners are aware that these processes are transformational, but there is no clear evidence to give guidance on how to maximise opportunities for the various parties. Little broad-based research exists in the field of application of restorative processes in different contexts. Few studies have investigated the needs, suspicions and assumptions of other vested-interest groups.

In *Integrating a Victim Perspective within Criminal Justice*, Lode Walgrave (Walgrave 2000) speaks of the work that needs to be done in the future. Most of what he says would be endorsed from a practitioner's view. Restorative interventions in conjunction with other necessary inter-agency inputs could engender a much more positive, constructive, future-focused process than the negative, punitive, backward-looking adversarial process that exists now. This is a challenge for the new National Probation Service.

In the introduction to her second draft of *A New Choreography* (2000) Ethnie Wallis, Director Designate of the Probation Services for England and Wales, states 'there is no such thing as a victimless crime. Probation staff will not collude with offenders about the degree of harm they have done and the impact of their crime on the lives and wellbeing of others'. She goes on to make reference to positively encouraging restorative approaches, acknowledging their developmental place in the work of the Service's National Directorate.

Properly undertaken, longer-term research by informed and respected researchers knowledgeable about the field could offer much in terms of guiding practice, and this could offer invaluable insights into managing change. Many of the major problems in developing new work are associated with management, internal agency cultures and the natural resistance to change. Training on working in victim contact and restorative work, currently provided by the Youth Justice Board nationally to aid implementation of the new youth legislation, has failed to attract a viable proportion of managers. It has been viewed as cascade training for practitioners. Implementation is in the management range, and it is unrealistic to expect learning to cascade upwards.

The new probation service will be a very different service from the one joined by the writer in 1985. It is today more clearly concerned with public protection and community safety. Direct work with victims is the strongest application of these concepts in practice, offering repair to victims (and offenders) in a variety of senses. All reparative work must primarily focus on victims – although undoubtedly, if offenders have been given the opportunity and support required to effect genuine repair, it is highly unlikely that they and their communities will not benefit too. The probation service, with these principles at its core, stands to be more effective and positive in its approach. Throughout all work with offenders the focus on victim perspectives (not least by offenders themselves) will lead to the more realistic, holistic overview of cases. The importance of harnessing the most productive blend of interventions then becomes more evident and practicable.

References

ACOP/Victim Support (1996) *The Release of Prisoners – Informing, Consulting and Supporting Victims.* London: ACOP/VS.

Dignan J. (2000) *Youth Justice Pilots Evaluation: Interim Report on Reparative Work and Youth Offending Teams.* London: HMSO.

HMIP (2000) *Thematic Inspection Report. The Victim Perspective: Ensuring the Victim Matters.* London: Home Office.

Home Office (1990) *Victim's Charter: A Statement of the Rights of Victims of Crime.* London: Home Office Public Relations Branch.

Home Office (1996) *The Victim's Charter: A Statement of Service Standards for Victims of Crime.* London: Home Office Communications Directorate.

Marshall T. and Merry S. (1990) *Crime and Accountability.* London: HMSO.

Walgrave L. (2000) 'Extending the victim perspective towards a systematic restorative justice alternative.' In A. Crawford and J. Goodey, *Integrating a Victim Perspective within Criminal Justice.* Dartmouth: Ashgate.

Wallis E. (2000) *A New Choreography – Integrated Strategy for the National Probation Service for England and Wales. Strategic Framework 2001–2004.* Draft 2 Consultation Document, November. London: Home Office.

Youth Justice Board (2001) *Good Practice Guidelines for Restorative Work with Victims and Young Offenders.* London: YJB.

9.

Victim Impact Statements

Voices to be Heard in the Criminal Justice Process?

Sandra Walklate

'I could not believe the judge had actually listened to what I had to say.'
(witness, quoted by Erez 1999, p.553)

Introduction

Many different kinds of endeavours have been put in place to secure a voice
for the victim of crime since the observation made by Schafer (1968) that
victims were the 'forgotten' party of the criminal justice system. Of course,
the accuracy of that original observation is a moot point, but it is nevertheless
the case that since the early 1980s the rhetorical and the actual presence of
the victim of crime has never been more keenly felt. However, there is still
some considerable debate surrounding the question of how best to ensure
that the presence of the crime victim is felt and under what circumstances.
That debate is nowhere more hotly contested, at least in the United
Kingdom, than in the arena surrounding the usefulness and value of the
victim impact statement. The purpose of this chapter is to explore that debate
and to examine its implications. In the process we will consider the overall
context of how best to take account of the victim of crime, if at all, within the
criminal justice system. In addition, we will identify the different ways in
which victim impact statements have been deployed. Moreover, we will
consider the implications of these different strategies for practitioners within

the criminal justice system. Finally we will explore the implications that the implementation of initiatives such as these have for our understanding of the central purpose of the criminal justice system.

What is a victim impact statement?

Victim impact statements accept that there is space for the victim of crime to have 'procedural rights' within the criminal justice process. Those in favour of the introduction of such statements broadly fall into that camp which supports the re-integration of the victim into the criminal justice process through greater participation in that process. Frequently, however, there have also been more obviously pragmatic reasons for moving in this direction. The need to secure the co-operation of victims, especially as witnesses, in the pursuit of the business of the criminal justice system counts as one important one. (See, for example, Justice 1998). So what is a victim impact statement and where does a practice like this sit with these broader concerns for re-integration?

The Community Law Reform Committee of Australia (1998, p.1) defines a victim impact statement in the following way:

> A victim impact statement is a statement setting out the full effects – physical, psychological, financial and social – suffered by a victim as a result of a crime. The statement is prepared for placement before the court engaged in sentencing an offender for the crime in question so that the court may fully understand the effects of the crime on the victim.

Of course, in some respects, this is a very general definition. For example, it gives no indication of whether or not such statements should be mandatory, neither does it say whether or not they should include recommendations for sentencing. Yet, despite such lack of clarity and precision concerning the place and the purpose of such measures there have been recent moves to introduce them into the criminal justice process in England and Wales. The question is: why?

In some respects it may be argued that the opportunity for putting a crime's full effect on the victim before the court already exists in the English and Welsh legal system. This is possible, for example, in the context of a plea for compensation or, in the case of a violent crime, in relation to injuries caused as a result of the victimisation put as evidence before the court. Nevertheless we have witnessed a slow but sure move towards putting in place more formal mechanisms to ensure the victim's voice is more clearly heard. With this in mind, pilot victim impact statement schemes were established in three police force areas in 1997 to encourage victims of all kinds of crimes to describe how the crime had affected them. These schemes are reported to be going nationwide in 2001. As the former Home Secretary Jack Straw is reported as saying, this would:

> give victims a voice in a way that they have not had before. It will be a real opportunity to make their views known more formally to the police, Crown Prosecution Service and the courts and to know they will be taken into account in the case. I want victims to feel they are at the heart of the criminal justice system. (*The Guardian*, 27 May, 2001 p.6)

In some respects statements like these raise the spectre of victim-led justice Saudi-Arabian style, which does not quite gel with traditional conceptions of justice associated with the criminal justice system of England and Wales. As Mawby and Gill (1987, pp.229–230) pointed out some time ago:

> to re-orientate the system towards a mandatory focus on victims' perspectives and the impact of crime is misconceived, both because it invites injustice (where the impact of crime is unrelated to criminal intent) and because it ignores the fact that many crimes are the concern of the state as well as the victim. (Mawby and Gill 1987, pp.229–30)

Despite inherent difficulties such as these for some commentators and certainly for some politicians, victim impact statements appear to be a 'good' thing insofar as they constitute another step on the road to victims' rights, at the maximum, and improved victim participation in the criminal justice system, at the minimum. This is a road, however, which was signposted by the politicisation of the victim (Miers 1978) quite some time ago and is now clearly mapped as part of any vote-winning strategy. So are victim impact statements yet another ploy in the symbolic invocation of the victim, on which politicians now so readily call? This is a question that we will return to, but first it is important to consider the extent to which the introduction of victim impact statements raises fundamental questions concerned with conceptions of justice, implementation and participation. It must be remembered that in the UK context the purpose is not explicitly to inform sentencing outcome, yet, despite this, questions associated with conceptions of justice remain. Drawing on the international evidence available we shall discuss each of the questions suggested above in turn.

Victim impact statements and the question of justice

The introduction of victim impact statements constitutes only one of a number of different ways in which the whole question of the victim's greater participation in the criminal justice process raises the question of what is the central purpose of that process. Conventional views of the adversarial system of justice within England and Wales would start from the view that its central purpose is to ensure both the structure and the function of the criminal trial. The second of these is perhaps the most telling in its consequences for all participants. McBarnett expressed this in this way:

> The civil trial takes the form of victim v. offender, but the criminal trial takes the form of state v. offender. The offence is not just against the victimised person, the offence is against the state. The state is not just the arbiter in a trial between victim and offender; the state is the victim... If victims feel that nobody cares about their suffering, it is in part because institutionally nobody does. (McBarnett 1988, p.300)

Thus, in principle, those who withhold evidence or refuse to give evidence, or in any way try to subvert the course of justice, may be prosecuted. The legal powers of the courts must be seen to be upheld despite the wishes of any other parties concerned. In this interpretation of the function of the criminal justice system, neither complainant nor defendant has much of a voice at all, though defendants have clearly more 'rights' in this context than complainants. From this point of view, then, extending the participation of the complainant in the criminal justice process must always be balanced by the matter of ensuring that the 'rights' of the defendant are not eroded. Ashworth (1993, 2000) has been a particularly vocal critic of the introduction of victim impact statements in this latter respect, especially in the use of them to inform sentencing.

If victim impact statements are used to inform sentencing, serious alarm bells are raised for those committed to the principle of the adversarial system: they argue that this is a tactic that potentially can introduce a level of arbitrariness to the sentencing process above and beyond that which already exists – since, in essence, sentencing becomes dependent upon the persuasive power of the victim's statement and the efficiency and accuracy with which it has been recorded. In other words, in principle setencing becomes subject to the potential influence of factors above and beyond the particular set of events before the court. It is in this sense that victim impact statements, if used in this way, might erode the rights of the offender to a 'fair' trial, lead to the imposition of heavier penalties than might otherwise have been the case, and result in an increase in sentencing disparity. The statement schemes introduced into England and Wales are not intended to influence sentencing, though this does not mean that greater awareness of the impact of a crime put before a court would not result in some of these effects (though it has to be said that victim impact statements are not the only source of arbitrariness in sentencing outcome). In some respects the potential for this already exists, sentencing tariff systems notwithstanding – which leads to the second issue to be addressed here. This issue draws our attention to the difference between this 'in principle' kind of argument and the issues that emerge at the level of practice.

Victim impact statements and the question of implementation

As the previous discussion has suggested, issues of practice can and do overtake questions of principle. This is nowhere more the case than when new measures are introduced into the repertoire of any organisation, and the criminal justice system is no different in this respect. Victim impact statements can take various forms and can be implemented in a number of different ways. Examples of such variations can be found across international jurisdictions. So what kind of statements are collected, and how, by whom, for what offences, and at what juncture in the proceedings, are all issues for consideration. The practical response to each of these questions seems to vary, depending upon the purpose of collecting the statement. However, outside of Canada, there has been very little systematic research that has reliably evaluated schemes that have been implemented in different ways.

Canadian research suggests that there are two sets of purposes for collecting victim impact statements. The first, identified as direct purposes, assume that such statements would provide an instrument to give information to the court; provide direct input by victims into the sentencing process; and assist the court in arriving at an 'appropriate' sentence. The second set, identified as indirect purposes, would provide a means for victims to offer direct input about the effects of an offence; increase victims' willingness to co-operate with the criminal justice; enhance victims' feelings of involvement and thereby improve victim satisfaction. That same research suggests that victims are more likely to participate in either kind of scheme if they are personally interviewed, and unlikely to participate if they think the offence minor, if they want to put the incident behind them, or if they are just too busy. Canadian schemes also seem to favour the police collecting such statements because of the benefits that seem to accrue from that for all parties. In other words, the police learned more about the crime and victims were more likely to feel that they were taken seriously. The actual use of the statements themselves seemed to vary according to whether the Crown Counsel thought that the impact was significant or not, and whether or not oral evidence had already covered the same material. Moreover, this research suggests that there was little difference in levels of satisfaction experienced by victims, whether or not their statement was used in court. Indeed, the improved levels of satisfaction reported by all victims who participated in such schemes were not necessarily related to the victim impact statement itself but to how victims felt they had been treated in general by the criminal justice process.

Less systematic research conducted in other countries would seem to support these overall conclusions, and also offers some evidence to allay the fears associated with the sentencing process, alluded to in the previous discussion. In this latter respect Erez (1999), for example, reports that victim impact statements are more likely to underestimate the impact of a crime than to overestimate it because 'stories are often constructed to suit the goals and objectives of the mediating agency' (*ibid.* p.550). Moreover, Erez and Rogers, reporting from an Australian study, assert:

> The study reveals a rich and varied repertoire of strategies used by the legal profession to maintain their autonomous status, circumvent external demands to consider victim input and justify overlooking concrete presentations of harm. Built-in organisational incentives to exclude victims, or proceed with minimal input from them, maintain and reinforce the traditional criminal justice approach to victims as an 'extraneous party' if not sheer 'troublemakers'. (Erez and Rogers 1999, p.234)

So it would seem, even where it is possible for victim impact statements to have an effect, that this is not necessarily the guaranteed outcome. Ashworth (2000) argues that raising victim expectations that are not met in this way might also be considered harmful. Yet it would seem that victims operate with quite a realistic set of expectations when participating in the criminal justice system in this way. Hoyle *et al.* (1998), reporting on the evaluation of the pilot statement schemes in England and Wales, suggest that people had mixed motives for participating in the scheme. Sixty per cent wanted to 'get things off their chest', 55 per cent wanted to affect the sentence, and 43 per cent wanted to give as much evidence as they could. Overall the majority felt satisfied with having participated, a factor contributing, in the view of Erez (1999), to the need for a 'therapeutic jurisprudence'. Or, as she states: 'Proceedings which provide victims with a voice or "process control" enhance their satisfaction with justice and sense of fair treatment' (*ibid.* p.551).

Sanders concludes that:

> Statement schemes are almost entirely unsuccessful in providing instrumental benefits for criminal justice agencies. Few victims feel more kindly

disposed to the criminal justice system as a result of their participation, since many statement schemes take an extra statement and then ignore the victim as comprehensively as ever. The criminal justice system remains mysterious and unwelcoming to most victims. (Sanders 1999, p.4)

If one takes a purely instrumental view of victim impact schemes and victims' involvement in them, then such a conclusion might be reached. However, despite the patchy and relatively unsystematic evidence available, this discussion has suggested that the picture might not be quite so straightforward for either the victim or the criminal justice system. There are clearly issues here for practitioners to consider, centring on such questions as who takes the statement, how it is done, where it is done, and how it is brought to the attention of the court. However, these issues, and the patchy findings which have been referred to in this discussion, raise the more general question of how to manage victim participation in the criminal justice process, since such participation does seem to have a therapeutic effect, the presence or absence of victim impact statements notwithstanding.

Victim impact statements and the question of participation

The introduction of victim impact statements is a measure that is largely associated with a 'victim allocution' model of the criminal justice system rather than a conventional model (*qua* Cavadino and Dignan 1996, p.234). These models are assumed to have not only different but also contradictory underlying philosophies and aims. Put simply, the first, conventional model is one rooted in conceptions of just deserts, in which the main victim measure is the compensation order and the role of the victim is considered minimal except when he or she is required as a witness. On the other hand, the second, victim allocution model is concerned with victim empowerment, in which victims' wishes are considered paramount in prosecution and sentencing decisions. The differences between these two models are felt most keenly in relation to the question of victim impact statements. Moreover, these differences, as we have seen, have been debated for the most part in connection with the victim's role in the sentencing process. In practical terms in England and

Wales this controversy has been avoided by not including that in the introduction of the measures referred to above. However, what cannot be avoided
are the inevitable tensions generated by the proposed introduction of a
measure which presumes a very different mode of victim participation within
the criminal justice system. While on the one hand the evidence suggests
some therapeutic value in such involvement, the question remains as to how
best to ensure victim participation in the criminal justice system – assuming
that we accept such participation as a 'good' idea.

Again, some time ago Mawby and Gill (1987, p.229) argued that there
were at least four aspects of victims' rights which could be developed: the
right to play an active role in the criminal justice process; the right to knowledge; the right to financial help; and the right to advice and support. While
interest in, and campaigns for, the victim of crime have proceeded apace since
these suggestions were made, arguably much could still be done to secure
these 'rights'. It is interesting to note that Mawby and Gill's proposals leave
the conventional model of criminal justice untouched. In the years since their
proposals much has been made, in debates around the nature and purpose of
criminal justice systems, of the value of moving towards an integrative, restorative justice model (Cavadino and Dignan 1996). This model takes reparation, reintegration of the offender, victim empowerment and human rights
as its aims, with a role for the victim that requires their active involvement.
Indeed, in Sanders' (1999) review of victim participation schemes for the
Scottish Office, it is only those schemes that either involve an 'auxiliary prosecutor' or are restorative in content, that afford the genuine opportunity for
victim participation. And while the Crime and Disorder Act 1998 makes
much of introducing mediation and reparation, especially in dealing with
young offenders, these remain measures that are 'added on' to a system
rooted in a different philosophy of justice.

This is not the place to discuss the relative strengths and weaknesses of
different models of justice, neither is it the place to consider how to trans-
form one model into another. However, this discussion does offer a perspective on the likely success or failure of victim impact statements as a measure

with which government policy is proceeding. Moreover, it also provides some clues as to why the research done on this issue offers the findings that it does.

The victim personal statement scheme

An interesting variation on the victim impact statement was introduced into the criminal justice process in England and Wales in November 2000. This, the 'victim personal statement' scheme, follows the spirit, if not the actual practice, of victim impact statements as discussed above. The purpose of a victim personal statement is twofold: first, to offer the crime victim the optional opportunity of relating to all the agencies concerned how a crime has affected them; and second, to provide the criminal justices agencies with more information about the impact of a crime. As already stated, this is an entirely optional scheme and is not intended to be used by the criminal justice agencies to affect sentencing outcome. It is intended as a two-stage process. The first stage is to be implemented separately, at the same time as the victim's witness statement is taken. The second stage allows the victim to describe the impact of any longer-term effects of the crime. Both statements are to form part of the case papers for any trial and it is seen as the responsibility of the police to collect both. These statements will provide an opportunity for victims to raise any concerns that they may have about aspects of the crime and the offender not dealt with elsewhere by the criminal justice process (like bail proceedings, for example), and will provide all agencies within the criminal justice process with more information; but this will only be the case if the victim chooses to make, and the police pursue, such statements. It remains to be seen how effective this scheme proves to be. However, in view of the previous discussion, it is likely that the underlying issues of justice, implementation and participation will remain.

Conclusion: making sense of structures, policies and processes

In some respects this discussion has struggled to unravel the debate around the value or otherwise of victim impact statements, largely because encapsulated within the introduction of this one measure are a range of more fundamental concerns about the victim in the criminal justice process. The evidence seems to suggest that any measure which takes care to pay attention to the needs and feelings of the crime victim will result in improved levels of satisfaction with the criminal justice system for those who participate in it. Victim impact statements are just one measure among many which may have this effect. This does not necessarily entail a questioning of the conventional purposes for criminal justice. Indeed, it has been suggested that such purposes can for the most part remain untouched, and victims of crime will still express greater satisfaction. So while this debate clearly relates to and articulates some of the tensions between different structural conceptions of justice, and as a policy may be implemented more or less effectively in a myriad of different ways, we are left with the evidence which points to gaps between structure and policy. We are left with processes. What is it that victims of crime, or anyone else who comes into to contact with the workings of the criminal justice system (or any other organisational setting for that matter), want from their contact with that organisation? In order to offer one answer to this question it will be useful to situate the discussion about this particular measure within a broader contextual framework.

During the 1990s there has emerged an increasingly diverse range of voices, all claiming to speak for the victim of crime. A common thread in this emergent concern, whether the victim is construed as the innocent victim of violent crime of the 1960s, the consumer of police services of the 1980s, or the secondary victim of crime of the 1990s, is the increasing consistency with which this victim is invoked as the symbolic person for whom we should all care. How that care might be construed has been differently informed, according to the kind of crime under discussion and the impact that such crime is presumed to have. So 'domestic' violence requires a differently informed response than murder, for example. Yet arguably the requirement for difference has been exaggerated, at the expense of appreciating the sameness of such experiences. This is not to downgrade the impact that traumatic events have on people's lives but simply to observe that while individually oriented practice may be able to take account of the differential impact of different crimes, policy cannot. How to respond then? By ensuring respect.

It should not be forgotten that victims of any kind of crime are people trying to deal with more or less exceptional circumstances in their lives. Some of those circumstances they may feel responsible for, some they may feel are shared with others, some have just happened to them (qua Harre, and Secord 1978). How they deal with such circumstances will depend in part upon their own personal resources, the personal resources of those close to them and the kind of support that they may or may not be offered by the various agencies with whom they have contact. Treating people with respect; that is, as individuals with personal resources, is a key mechanism for ensuring that, traumatic circumstances notwithstanding, they are enabled to make use of their resources to make sense of what has happened in their lives. How they might choose to do that is likely to be infinitely variable. Working with an understanding of the search for respect as a key human condition is the clear and central message of Harre's work (1979).

There are a number of implications that can be derived from the position outlined above. For example, this position challenges any presumed special status to be assigned to the victim of crime. This does not mean to say that such crime does not impact upon people; it does. But it does imply that in terms of practice it is useful to remember that 'victims' are people. In other words, whether male or female, black or white, old or young; the maintenance of respect and the avoidance of contempt is key to making people feel OK; a way of sustaining their sense of wellbeing rather than abusing or undermining it. In other words, in the face of increasing diversity and the celebration of difference, there may be still some value in working with, exploring, and learning from, the commonalities inherent in the human condition. The search for respect, arguably, is one of these. So when people express greater satisfaction with their involvement in the criminal justice process, whatever form that involvement has taken, they may simply be expressing the view that they have been treated as people. People, yes, with fads, foibles and particular points of view, but nevertheless as people with rights. One of those rights is to be treated with respect. The demand to be heard within the criminal justice process may be no more and no less than this; hence the quote from Erez' paper with which this chapter began. In other words, there may be no need for yet more measures to improve the indirect benefits of victim participation. Those benefits are already achievable. However, as Mawby and Gill stated:

> If victims are indeed the forgotten people of the welfare state, it would be a double irony were they to become, in the late 1980s, the victims of political expediency. (Mawby and Gill 1987, p.4)

Arguably, for lack of a full and informed debate about the central purpose of the victim impact statement in the context of the criminal justice system in England and Wales, that is what the victims of crime have now become.

References

Ashworth A. (1993) 'Victim impact statements and sentencing.' *Criminal Law Review,* 498–509.

Ashworth A. (2000) 'Victims' rights, defendants' rights and criminal procedure.' In A. Crawford and J. Goodey (eds.) *Integrating a Victim Perspective within Criminal Justice: International Debates.* Aldershot: Ashgate.

Cavadino M. and Dignan J. (1996) 'Towards a framework for conceptualising and evaluating models of criminal justice from a victim's perspective.' *International Review of Victimology* 4, 3, 153–182.

Community Law Reform Committee of Australia (1998) http://www.dpa.act.gov.au/ag/Reports/CLRC/r6/Report6c3.html

Erez E. (1999) 'Who's afraid of the big bad victim? Victim impact statements as victim empowerment and enhancement of justice.' *Criminal Law Review,* 545–556.

Erez E. and Rogers L. (1999) 'Victim impact statements and sentencing outcomes and processes: the perspectives of legal professionals.' *British Journal of Criminology* 39, 2, Spring, 216–239.

Harre, R. (1979) *Social Being.* Oxford: Basil Blackwell.

Harre, R. and Secord P.F. (1978) *The Explanation of Social Behaviour.* Oxford: Basil Blackwell.

Hoyle C., Cape E., Morgan R. and Sanders A. (1998) *Evaluation of the One-Stop Shop and Victim Statement Pilot Projects. A Report for the Home Office Research and Development Statistic Directorate.* Bristol: Department of Law, University of Bristol.

Justice (1998) *Victims in Criminal Justice. Report of the Committee on the Role of the Victim in Criminal Justice.* London: Justice.

McBarnett, D. (1988) 'Victim in the witness box – confronting victimology's stereotype.' *Contemporary Crises* 7, 279–303.

Mawby R. and Gill M. (1987) *Crime Victims: Needs, Services and the Voluntary Sector.* London: Tavistock.

Miers D. (1978) *Responses to Victimisation.* Abingdon: Professional Books.

Sanders A. (1999) *Taking Account of Victims in the Criminal Justice System: A Review of the Literature.* Edinburgh: Scottish Office Central Research Unit: Social Work Findings No. 32.

Shafer S. (1968) *The Victim and His Criminal.* New York: Random House.

10

Addressing Victim Issues in Pre-Sentence Reports

Jane Dominey

Introduction

The pre-sentence report (PSR) is the document in which a probation officer provides the sentencing court with an analysis and assessment of the defendant's offence and personal circumstances. It may also propose that the court imposes a probation order, community service order or other community penalty. For the youth courts a probation officer, social worker or other member of the youth offending team writes PSRs. The history and changing emphasis of PSRs is outlined by Smith (1996).

In Scotland the equivalent report is the social enquiry report, and is prepared by a social worker specialising in criminal justice issues employed by the local authority.

This chapter seeks to describe how the PSR has developed in response to the developing interest in and concern for the victim of crime (Walklate 1989; Zedner 1997). The structure of the PSR is now dictated by national standards issued by the Home Office. Following an account of the ways in which national standards deal with victim issues, attention is given to how report authors work in practice.

The chapter also considers ways in which practitioners can assess the extent of awareness of and empathy for victims in the offenders with whom they work. It is argued that PSR practice sensitive to the position of victims has improved the way that probation officers work with incidents of domestic violence and identify patterns of offending such as racially motivated assaults.

There is little empirical evidence that offenders who display an increased empathy for their victims have a corresponding reduction in their likelihood of re-offending. The need for further research into the areas of remorse and victim awareness is highlighted. Training for PSR authors is also identified as necessary if practice in this area is to continue to develop.

The chapter concludes with suggested guidelines for good practice.

What do national standards require of PSRs?

The 1992 national standards for the supervision of offenders in the community in England and Wales require PSRs to include a section about the current offence. In this section, the author is directed to summarise 'the facts and seriousness of the offence(s), including aggravating and mitigating factors known to the report writer and the offender's attitude to the offence(s)'. Although the 1992 standards do make reference to the victims of crime elsewhere, including reference to the victim is not a requirement of the PSR.

A revised set of national standards was issued in 1995 and the growing political concern about victims of crime is reflected in the greater prominence given to victims throughout. The 1995 standards require PSRs to contain a section headed 'offence analysis' and list points to be included in the analysis, among them:

> an assessment of the consequences of the offence, **including the impact on the victim** as set out in victim statements or other papers available from the Crown Prosecution Service (CPS) or the damage otherwise done by the offence
>
> **an assessment of the offender's attitude to the victim and awareness of its consequences** drawing attention to any evidence of acceptance or minimisation of responsibility, remorse or guilt and any expressed desire to make amends. (Home Office 1995, pp.9–10; original highlighting)

This emphasis on the defendant's attitude to the victim as well as to the crime continues in the current set of national standards which was issued in 2000. Again, the PSR author is required to assess both the impact of the offence on the victim and the offender's attitude to the victim. Additionally, the report writer is asked to indicate whether the offender has undertaken any reparation for the crime (Home Office 2000a).

The preparation of PSRs for the youth court is subject to the national standards for youth justice. These include a similar requirement for PSR authors to comment on what is known about the impact of the offence on the victim and to assess the defendant's awareness of the consequences of the offence for any victims. Given the emphasis on reparation in youth justice policy, the standards also include a section on work with victims of crime, and guidelines for communicating with victims, obtaining their consent and protecting their confidentiality when considering reparation orders and other disposals involving some element of direct reparation (Youth Justice Board 2000). The Youth Justice Board is also producing a guide to good practice in the area of restorative work and young offenders.

In Scotland, where the local authorities provide criminal justice social work services, social enquiry reports (SERs) are the documents written for the courts with the intention of providing information about offenders and assisting sentencing. A framework of national standards, the most recent set of which was issued in 2000, governs this work. These standards, which are longer and contain considerably more guidance about report-writing practice than the English and Welsh equivalent, do also highlight the need to take account of the position of the victim. In the guidance for the content of the SER interview, the social worker is told to explore

> the offender's attitude to and explanation for his or her offending including his or her perceptions of its seriousness and its consequences for others including any victim (para.2.8.1)

and

how the offender feels about the offending. Does he or she express any genuine remorse or concern for the victim? (para. 2.8.4) (Scottish Executive 2000)

What do PSR authors do in practice?

PSR authors are therefore charged with the job of informing the court about the consequences of the offence for the victim and the extent to which the offender understands these consequences and feels remorseful. This is a complex task and there are several practical factors which have an impact on the quality of the completed piece of work.

PSRs in England and Wales are required to be completed within at most 15 working days of request and so the PSR author has limited time to undertake a range of enquiries, gather the required information and make an informed assessment. An interview with the offender is the key element of the process. National standards recommend 'at least one face-to-face interview with the offender' (para B4) and in practice the vast majority of PSRs are completed after a single interview.

Scottish standards do not set a period of time in which reports must be prepared, but do require that they 'reach the clerk of court by midday on the working day before the court hearing or, if possible, sooner' (para. 6.7, Scottish Executive 2000). A second interview with the defendant is recommended in a range of circumstances, including interviewing family members or visiting the offender at home.

PSR authors also have access to a pack of information supplied by the Crown Prosecution Service (CPS), including statements of witnesses, police interviews and details of the defendant's previous convictions. If the CPS pack has not reached the PSR author prior to the interview, then the interviewer must manage without details of the offence, its victims and the explanations given by the offender when interviewed by the police. This information highlights important areas for questioning and enables contradictions in the account given at the PSR interview to be identified and explored.

The late arrival of CPS packs has a significant impact on the quality of PSR interviews and, in particular, means that the PSR author is entirely reliant on the offender for information about the victim of the offence. This issue was identified in the report from the Probation Inspectorate, *The Victim Perspective: Ensuring the Victim Matters* which found that as many as 50 per cent of CPS packs were arriving late. PSR authors also reported that, even when they did have information from the CPS, specific detail about the 'effect of the offence on the victim was often very slim' (Home Office 2000b). The Inspectorate did accept that probation services were working with the CPS to improve the quality and timeliness of information provided, with some evidence of success.

In those areas where victim personal statements are prepared these are available to PSR authors and provide specific information about the impact of the offence on the victim. Direct contact with the police officer in the case can also offer the probation officer access to additional information about the offence and the circumstances of the victim. Such contact, in the case of serious offences and high risk offenders, is commended by the Inspectorate report. This communication is an example of the greater flow of information between these two agencies, which has now spread beyond issues of public protection and the management of those offenders assessed as dangerous.

Where the subject of the PSR is an adult, PSR authors only rarely make direct contact with victims. An example of such contact is provided by a scheme in West Yorkshire, referred to in the Inspectorate report, in which a specialist worker from the probation service victim unit interviews women who have been assaulted by their male partners. A report about issues for the victim is then prepared for the PSR author. Such an approach in cases of domestic violence is also advocated in guidelines issued by the National Association of Probation Officers (NAPO),

> Offer the victim/survivor an appointment either at home or at the probation office and inform the perpetrator that this will be done; in order to verify the information and take all possible steps for the protection of the victim(s)/ survivor(s). (NAPO 1998, p.11)

Scottish standards for SERs explicitly recommend this practice.

> In cases of domestic violence, report writers should, with her consent, interview the woman partner to establish how the current offence may or may not fit into a pattern of abusive behaviour (this interview should be conducted separately from the male offender). They should also contact the police with a view to establishing whether there have been any call-outs to the address alleging abuse. (Scottish Executive 2000, para.3.12.6)

Such an approach is not without its critics. Teft (1998), drawing on his experience as a probation officer specialising in domestic violence work, argues strongly that there should be no question of direct contact between report writers and victims of domestic violence. He stresses that the woman should not be put in the position of having to give repeated accounts of her experience to successive representatives of the criminal justice system. He identifies the risk of the woman choosing to minimise the seriousness of the violence, either as a result of pressure from the perpetrator or out of a desire to resume the relationship. He also highlights a range of difficulties associated with home visits, for example, the difficulty of ensuring privacy, the problem of the arrival home of the perpetrator during the interview, particularly if in breach of bail conditions, and the more general safety risk associated with home visits at the PSR stage. Teft accepts that the NAPO guidelines include caveats and warnings intended to address these points, but believes that they do not go far enough. As an alternative, he offers his own suggestions for the improvement of PSR practice with regard to victims. He reminds PSR authors that background information, for example, about any history of police call-outs, cautions and charges withdrawn, can be obtained from police domestic violence units. He also identifies a frequent gap in the information provided by the CPS.

> Crown Prosecution papers often omit medical reports, particularly the body diagram indicating where injuries were caused. I would urge report writers to obtain copies of these before commencing their reports. (Teft 1998, p.227)

In a wide-ranging discussion of the position of victims in the criminal justice system (JUSTICE 1998), the organisation JUSTICE considered whether direct contact between victims and PSR authors would provide sentencers with a clearer understanding of the effect and impact of the crime. It concluded that this was not the way forward.

> We do not feel that the pre-sentence report writer can be expected to carry the burden both of reporting on the offender and of conveying information relating to victims in the one report. (JUSTICE 1998, p.91)

The JUSTICE report commented more favourably on the use of victim impact statements as a means of ensuring that the voice of the victim is heard in court proceedings (see Chapter 9).

In contrast, as a consequence of the new orders available to youth courts, workers in youth offending teams (YOTs) do have direct contact with victims of crime at the PSR stage. This contact seeks to establish the attitude of the victim to receiving reparation from the young person responsible for the offence. Such reparation could be carried out under the terms of a reparation order or as part of other disposals such as action plan or supervision orders.

Reparation orders are a new development in the fast-changing world of youth offending (Williams 2000). At this early stage it appears that the business of contacting victims is undertaken in a variety of ways. In some areas this task rests with police officers working within YOTs on the basis that the police have a history of working with victims. In other areas this task is shared with probation officer and social worker team members, recognising the skills and experience that they bring to this work. YOTs are also required by the Youth Justice Board to enter into joint working arrangements with Victim Support and other local victim organisations.

NACRO, a national voluntary organisation engaged in a wide variety of activities in the area of youth justice, has produced a valuable guide to the production of PSRs for the youth court (NACRO 2000). It suggests that in order to ensure some independence, the contact with the victim is made by a YOT member other than the PSR author. It recommends that this contact is not made until after the first interview between PSR author and young person so that the victim can be given a realistic impression of the offender's attitude to the offence and capacity to engage in various forms of reparation. The guide contains a thorough checklist of points to cover in interview with the victim, including what information to pass to the victim and the facts and opinions to be elicited.

The experience of one youth justice team, in which the police officer member of the team makes contact, is that when a victim is prepared to consider direct reparation, a face-to-face apology from the young person is the most commonly negotiated outcome. This youth offending team has worked with a variety of victims, including people who have been assaulted or who have had their property damaged, as well as managers of large city-centre stores. It is crucial that, at this early stage in the development of this work, practices are developed which meet the needs of victims for information and competence in the handling of 'their' cases. The satisfaction of victims with reparation work ordered by the youth courts will be an important area for future research.

Assessing victim awareness

In order to assess the extent to which defendants are aware of the consequences of their offences for their victims, PSR authors are therefore largely dependent on information gained at interview, supported by written information from the CPS and, in some areas, a victim impact statement.

Before considering how probation officers go about making this assessment, it is worth noting the complexity of crime and the fact that often a PSR author is presented with a case where there is not a straightforward relationship between one offender, one offence and one victim. In some offences, for example shoplifting from a chain store or fraudulently claiming benefit, a large commercial organisation or government department suffers the loss. Some defendants (examples include those prosecuted following inquiries into abuse in children's homes) have committed multiple offences with many victims. Offences such as possession of drugs for personal use and soliciting can be argued to be without victims. This point is argued further by Wasik

(1999) in an article considering the issues raised by reparation orders. He gives the example of a robbery from a corner shop, one small branch of a large trading corporation. He outlines the variety of potential victims in this case, including the shoppers in the store at the time of the robbery, the staff on duty and the store's owner, and asks which of these would qualify as victims and hence be eligible for reparation.

The first task for probation officers is, therefore, to make a decision about who or what in the case before them qualifies as a victim. This is a decision which will be informed by the worker's values and priorities. Different judgements would be reached (for example, in the case of a woman convicted of possessing a small amount of cannabis with intent to supply it within her own group of immediate friends) by probation officers who differed in their opinion about the legal position of cannabis.

Any assessment of the offender's awareness of the consequences of the offence for the victim is then likely to begin with some direct questioning about the offender's thinking about the victim, both at the time of the offence and subsequently. PSR authors may also present the defendant with information about the offence or victim contained in the CPS pack and ask for further explanation or comment. They may ask the offender to talk more generally about the experience of being a victim in order to make an assessment of the extent to which the offender understands the possible consequences of crime. An assessment based on information gathered in this way then appears in the PSR. Typical comments made about offenders may include that they demonstrate 'genuine remorse' or, in contrast, that they seem 'to regret the offence as it has led to a court appearance rather than because of the harm done to the victim'.

Some practical guidance, specifically for those working with men who sexually abuse, is provided by Briggs *et al.* (1997). They outline an assessment process beginning with gathering information from statements made by victims and witnesses. Suggested questions at interview include

'How have these events/allegations affected you?' 'How have they affected others in your family?' 'How have they affected those in the victim's family?' 'How have they affected those who have had to deal with the case?' 'What did you think/feel during the abuse?' 'What do you feel now?' 'What do you think your victim felt during the abuse and now?' (Briggs *et al.* 1998, p.121)

There are published scales and questionnaires intended to help measure the victim empathy of sexual abusers. These include the Levinson Victim Empathy Scale and the Carick-Adkerson Victim Empathy and Remorse Inventory (see Briggs *et al.* 1998 for further discussion).

There has been little or no research into the quality of assessments made by probation officers in the areas of remorse or victim awareness. Indeed, although remorse appears to be an important concept in criminal law, it appears to be little researched. Horne asks the following questions:

Does the intensity of remorse decline as time passes, and does its severity and duration depend on the extent of the harm that the offender has caused and how close he was to the victim? These are empirical questions that are yet to be studied. (Horne 1999, pp.24–25)

As a consequence, PSR authors are making these assessments without guidance about important issues such as whether saying sorry is a reliable indication of being sorry. The link between expressing remorse today and behaving better tomorrow is not established. It may be that articulate defendants are more likely to be able to convey expressions of remorse. Some offenders will anticipate that making an apology is expected of them. It is undoubtedly the case that the interaction between interviewer and interviewee is affected by dynamics arising from factors such as gender, race, class and age (Celnick and McWilliams 1995).

In their study of the effectiveness of victim-orientated legal reform in Europe, Brienen *et al.* (2000) highlight the importance of staff training in the improvement of services to victims. The quality of assessments made in PSRs will depend on the extent to which report writers have received training in the area of victimology. Some probation staff will be involved in the contact arrangements that provide information to, and seek the opinions of, the victims of those prisoners sentenced to at least 12 months in prison. Training was provided throughout the probation service at the time that this new work was taken on (Home Office 1996). Some report writers will transfer knowledge and skills from this aspect of probation practice or from experience elsewhere.

In 1998 the Home Office and the Association of Chief Officers of Probation jointly reviewed existing training arrangements for work with victims and made recommendations for future development in this area (Home Office/ACOP 1998). These recommendations include finding ways of incorporating victim concerns into PSR training. The report also highlighted the need for research into the effectiveness of current work with victims and for the development of long-term evaluative techniques for assessing the effectiveness of victim learning programmes and their impact on practice.

The inspection of work with victims undertaken by HM Inspectorate of Probation (HMIP) reported shortcomings and omissions in the training, development and supervision of staff working with victims and recommended that probation services assess the learning needs of all staff involved in victim contact work and devise a strategy to meet them.

The curriculum for the Diploma in Probation Studies, which since 1998 has been the professional qualification for probation officers, takes some limited account of victim issues. The National Vocational Qualification, which forms an integral part of the Diploma, requires candidates to demonstrate an understanding of the impact of crime on victims and their need for protection, respect, recognition and information. If these issues are given proper time and attention by those responsible for delivering training on Diploma in Probation Studies programmes, then newly qualified PSR writers will have a foundation understanding of victim issues in criminal justice. Occupational standards dealing specifically with victim contact work are also being developed and these will then be used to guide the development and appraisal of qualified staff practising in this area.

Increasing victim empathy

For those offenders who are sentenced to a community order (for example, probation or community service) or to a prison sentence that will result in a period of statutory supervision on their release, the PSR interview marks the start of their contact with the probation service. The framework set for work with offenders requires that supervision in the community shall 'challenge the offender to accept responsibility for the crimes committed and their consequences' (para. C8). Further, a written supervision plan will be completed for every offender addressing, amongst other things, 'where there has been a direct victim, work on the offender's attitude to victims, including specific attention to racially motivated offending' (para. C10, Home Office 2000a). Work done at the PSR stage to assess issues of victim awareness becomes, therefore, the start of a process intended to raise victim empathy in offenders.

A range of methods has been employed with the intention of increasing empathy with crime victims. Such work is done both with individual supervisees and in groupwork settings. One way of making a start with this work is to use the individual's own experience of being a victim, an approach which acknowledges that those on probation or in custody often find themselves in circumstances where they are victimised (Peelo and Stewart 1992; Webb and Williams 2000; Boswell 1995). Feelings associated with being a victim, such as shock, anger and guilt, are elicited and links can gradually be made with offences perpetrated.

Scenarios can be used to generate discussion about the consequences of crime for victims and to explore victims' needs for such things as apology, compensation, security and retribution. Video material, some of it produced by campaigning organisations such as the Campaign Against Drinking and Driving, can be used to give a clear and harrowing picture of the consequences of driving offences for bereaved families. In some groupwork programmes, group members are encouraged to write letters to their victims, which will not usually be sent, outlining their apologies and regret for their actions.

Some work with offenders tackles these issues in a more direct way. Groups have been run which bring offenders together with victims of crime. Launay (1985) writes about involving victims in some aspects of his work with prisoners at Rochester Youth Custody Centre. In a structured programme of discussion and role-play, a group of convicted burglars and victims referred from the local Victim Support scheme challenge each other's prejudices, stereotypes and rationalisations.

Nation and Arnott (1991) explain that their decision to include burglary victims in some sessions of their group programme for convicted burglars was on the basis that 'they alone were able to convey to burglars an awareness of the misery caused by house burglary' (p.63).

The Howard League undertook a study of work being done with prisoners on victim awareness issues (Howard League 1997). Some examples of good practice were identified, but the study concluded that the only example of properly structured work addressing victim issues was within the sex offender treatment programmes. Elsewhere it appeared that issues of victim awareness were being dealt with superficially.

What is the impact of these changes in practice?

It is appropriate to ask what has been achieved by the increasing profile of victim issues in the practice of PSR and SER preparation.

One positive consequence of paying proper attention to victim issues is that the PSR author is much better placed to identify important patterns of offending. Asking detailed questions about the current offence and about previous convictions can reveal a history of, for example, racially motivated offences, or other hate-based offending such as homophobic assaults, domestic violence or child abuse. Key areas for the report author to explore include information about current and past victims (e.g. age, gender, race, and relationship to the defendant) as well as more general details about the offences. Time can then be spent in interview examining these patterns and refining the assessment of the risk posed by the offender to potential future victims. Such an approach goes some way to answering criticisms that the criminal justice system makes only a minimal and limited response to the victim of crime (Walklate 1989).

It is implicit in much of the literature about victim awareness and victim empathy work that offenders who experience remorse or have a clear understanding of the impact of their behaviour on others are less likely to reoffend. The Howard League, in its study of victim awareness work in prison, takes this view. Work on issues relating to victims of crime is important because

> by ensuring that prisoners are aware of the impact of their crimes it may be a powerful motivator in reducing offending behaviour thereby creating fewer victims of crime in the future. (Howard League 1997, p.8)

The empirical basis for this claim does not seem clear. Horne (1999) draws attention to the lack of research into the concept of remorse. Underdown, in his study of the principles underpinning the effective supervision of offenders, considered the extent to which changes in attitude were correlated to reductions in reoffending. He found the association between the attitudinal component of CRIME-PICS (a tool designed to measure changes in attitude and beliefs in offenders which includes a victim-awareness component) and reduced reconviction to be less than certain:

> attitudinal measures are an important interim evaluation measure but they need to be used in tandem with reconvictions methods rather than instead of them. (Underdown 1998, p.119)

Encouraging offenders to think more seriously about the impact of their behaviour and increasing their awareness of the victims of crime could be argued to be a good thing in itself. However, without evidence of a link between remorse and a reduction of reoffending, work intended to raise the level of victim awareness displayed by offenders forms part of the drive to raise the profile of victims in the criminal justice system rather than an element of a strategy of evidence-based practice.

Developing future practice

The current political and policy climate places an increased emphasis on the victim perspective in criminal justice. National standards across the United Kingdom require report writers to address this issue. This chapter has sought to identify how report writers can practice in a way which is sensitive to the needs both of victim and offender, producing reports that deal with victim issues in a way which goes beyond paying lip-service to current concerns and preoccupations.

This chapter has also drawn attention to the need for empirical study into the identification and measurement of remorse and victim awareness. There is also scope for research into whether people who have a growing understanding of the impact of their criminal behaviour are less likely to offend in the future. This lack of knowledge about whether offenders who express an understanding of and regret for the consequences of their actions are less likely to reoffend should limit the confidence with which PSR authors claim the presence or absence of remorse as a key element of risk assessments. It also raises questions about the way in which the parole board relies on probation officers' judgements about regret and remorse in making decisions about whether prisoners can be released.

Training has been identified as crucial for probation staff who will have direct contact with victims, including those who will be making arrangements for reparation orders. Report writers too need input on crime and the impact of the criminal justice system from the victim's perspective if reports are to deal with these issues in a meaningful way.

The following points, emerging from some of the themes explored earlier in the chapter, provide an outline for good practice:

- Victim issues should be included in all training for PSR writers.

- PSR authors should obtain information about the offence and any victims from prosecution papers and, in some cases, sources such as specialist domestic violence units, racial harassment units or the police.

- In cases where the issues are complex (e.g. numerous victims, history of repeat victimisation, hate-based offending) it would be appropriate to seek extra time for completion of the report.

- Victim issues are more important to some reports than others. Remorse is more likely to be felt in cases where serious harm was caused. Some offences do not have direct victims and some have no victim at all.

- In interview with defendants, PSR authors should be aware that offenders may also have personal experience of loss, hurt and victimisation.

- When the victim is to be contacted at the PSR stage, full information needs to be provided about the process and the range of possible outcomes. Time needs to be allowed to ensure the victim's involvement is based on informed consent.

- Factors such as race, gender, class, disability and sexuality, which require sensitive handling at an initial interview, will have an impact on the offender and the victim's attitude to the offence, to the criminal justice system and to each other.

References

Boswell G. (1995) *Violent Victims.* London: The Prince's Trust.

Brienen M. *et al.* (2000) 'Evaluation and meta-evaluation of the effectiveness of victim-oriented legal reform in Europe.' *Criminologie* 33, 1, 122–144.

Briggs D. *et al.* (1997) *Assessing Men who Sexually Abuse.* London: Jessica Kingsley.

Celnick A. and McWilliams B. (1995) 'PSRs and National Standards: Who Calls the Tune?' In B. Williams (ed.) *Probation Values.* Birmingham: Venture.

Home Office (1992) *National Standards for the Supervision of Offenders in the Community.* London: Home Office.

Home Office (1995) *National Standards for the Supervision of Offenders in the Community.* London: Home Office.

Home Office (1996) *Training Materials for Contact with Victims.* London: Home Office Probation Training Unit.

Home Office (2000a) *National Standards for the Supervision of Offenders in the Community.* London: Home Office.

Home Office (2000b) *The Victim Perspective: Ensuring the Victim Matters.* London: HMIP [Website: http://homeoffice.gov.uk/hmiprob/themvict.htm]

Home Office/ACOP (1998) *The Review of Learning and Development Needs for Working with Victims and the Evaluation of Training Materials.* London: ACOP.

Horne A. (1999) 'Reflections on remorse in forensic psychotherapy.' In M. Cox (ed.) *Remorse and Reparation*. London: Jessica Kingsley.

Howard League (1997) *Are Prisoners Challenged on Victims of Crime?* London: Howard League.

JUSTICE (1998) *Victims in Criminal Justice*. London: JUSTICE.

Launay G. (1985) 'Bringing victims and offenders together: A comparison of two models.' *Howard Journal* 24, 3, 200–212.

NACRO (2000) *Pre-sentence Reports for Young People: A Good Practice Guide*. London: NACRO.

NAPO (1998) *Domestic Violence Policy and Practice Guidance*. London: NAPO.

Nation D. and Arnott J. (1991) 'House burglars and victims.' *Probation Journal* 38, 2, 68–74.

Peelo M. and Stewart J. (1992) 'Trashing and looting.' *Probation Journal* 39, 3, 138–142.

Scottish Executive (2000) *National Standards for Social Enquiry and Related Reports and Court Based Social Work Service*. Edinburgh: Scottish Executive.

Smith D. (1996) 'Pre-sentence Reports.' In T. May and A. Vass (eds.) *Working with Offenders: Issues, Contexts and Outcomes*. London: Sage.

Teft P. (1998) 'Should PSR writers be interviewing victims of domestic violence?' *Probation Journal* 45, 4, 226–227.

Underdown A. (1998) *Strategies for Effective Offender Supervision*. London: Home Office.

Walklate S. (1989) *Victimology: the Victim and the Criminal Justice System*. London: Unwin Hyman.

Wasik M. (1999) 'Reparation: Sentencing the victim.' *Criminal Law Review,* June, 470–479.

Webb D. and Williams B. (2000) 'Violent men in prison: Confronting offending behaviours without denying prior victimisation.' In H. Kemshall and J. Pritchard (eds.) *Good Practice in Working with Victims of Violence*. London: Jessica Kingsley.

Williams B. (2000) 'Victims of Crime and the New Youth Justice.' In B. Goldson (ed.) *The New Youth Justice*. Lyme Regis: Russell House.

Youth Justice Board (2000) *National Standards for Youth Justice*. London: Youth Justice Board. [Website: http: //youth-justice-board.gov.uk/policy/reference/html]

Zedner L. (1997) 'Victims.' In M. Maguire, R. Morgan and R. Reiner (eds.) *Oxford Handbook of Criminology*. Oxford: Oxford University Press.

II.

Effective Work with Abusive Men

Listening to Women

David Morran, Moira Andrew and Rory Macrae

The official 'discovery' of men's violence against their partners is compara-
tively recent in the UK (Bowker 1983). The problem of 'battered wives'
emerged gradually in the early 1970's (Dobash and Dobash 1979), to be
followed soon afterwards by that of 'battered babies'. In studying how these
phenomena were absorbed into public consciousness, Bruce (1979) has
compared the proceedings of the Select Committee on Violence in Marriage
(1975) with those of the Select Committee on Violence in the Family, which
took place the following year. Two distinct trends are apparent; the extent of
official ignorance about the nature and extent of violence against women,
and the considerable discrepancies in the evidence given by police and social
workers to the respective Select Committees. While the disapproval expressed about violence to children was strong and unanimous, the evidence
concerning violence against women was often equivocal. Robust and rapid
intervention was urged in cases relating to children, whereas caution and re-
straint were the watchwords as far as violence to women was concerned.

Throughout the 1970s and 1980s, as the issue of child care became a
major political concern and child protection cases increasingly assumed
priority on social workers' caseloads, service provision for women experiencing violence at the hands of their partners continued to be funded inconsis-
tently and at a basic level.

It is clear that while children are presumed to be the innocent victims of violence at the hands (usually) of violent men, the position of women victims of violence has continued to be viewed much more ambivalently. Wilson (1983) and Hanmer and Leonard (1984) point out that 'domestic violence' against women, which by its very nature is generally hidden from public view, has invariably been seen as a private matter because of widely held beliefs about family life. Pahl (1985) suggests that as concepts such as 'wife,' 'family,' 'home,' and 'private' are explicitly and implicitly linked, men's violence against women in the home was consequently viewed as being a different type of violence from that which occurred against children, between strangers or in the public domain.

It is significant that two 'experts' who presented evidence to the 1975 Committee, Erin Pizzey, then of Chiswick Women's Refuge, and psychiatrist John Gayford, spoke of women victims as being 'attracted' to violent partners, or 'prone to violence' (see Pizzey 1974; Gayford 1975, 1976). Beliefs that women are themselves to blame for being victims of domestic violence continue to be widespread among the general public, (Schlesinger *et al.* 1992) and are also shared by many social service professionals. Borkowski's study of doctors, solicitors, health visitors and social workers found that 'the personality of the woman consistently rates above the personality of the man as an explanation for the violence', (Borkowski, Murch and Walker 1983, p.60).

Seeking help: women's experience and agency responses

Several accounts have illustrated the general lack of comprehension, and unwillingness to become officially involved, which battered women have historically experienced from social workers, doctors, police and courts (Dobash and Dobash 1979; Binney *et al.* 1985; Gagnon and Lavoie 1990). Jan Pahl (1985) found, for example, that most of the women she interviewed in a women's refuge had sought help from a variety of sources including social workers, police and general practitioners and had invariably found them actively unhelpful.

Social workers have been particularly criticised for overlooking or disregarding women's accounts about experiencing domestic violence, focusing instead on the safety of any children in the home, and regarding the nuclear family unit as sacrosanct, frequently at a high cost to the women involved (Dobash and Dobash 1979; Borkowski *et al.* 1983; Maynard 1985).

Maynard's 1985 study of social work records found that social workers often failed to recognise when violence was actually occurring in cases they were dealing with, and when they did recognise that violence was taking place tended to refer to this only in passing, failing to deal with the issue directly. Maynard accuses social workers of accepting and colluding with men's explanations that women had provoked the 'deserved' violence as a result of their own personal or domestic 'inadequacies'. Social workers' overriding concerns, she argues, were invariably the welfare of children in households, and she cites instances of social workers dissuading women from leaving violent husbands by stressing the importance of the women's primary role as wives and mothers.

Equally trenchant criticisms have been levelled in the past at traditional police responses to domestic violence and at their general reluctance to intervene in what was frequently perceived to be a private family matter. (See for example Smith 1989; Dobash and Dobash 1992).

Throughout the 1990s, however, there has been considerable pressure on the police to adopt more proactive responses to the problem of men's violence in the home, and constabularies such as West Yorkshire, the London Metropolitan and Lothian and Borders have been energetic in increasing staff training and awareness, monitoring domestic violence callouts and establishing domestic violence units. In 1990 directives concerning enhanced police procedures were issued by the Home Office in England and Wales and by the Lord Advocate in Scotland. One of the main consequences of these directives is that women and men are now interviewed separately following domestic violence callouts.

Since Maynard conducted her social work study in the mid 1980s there has similarly been an enormous increase in social workers' awareness about violence which men commit against women partners *and* children, and in the development of stringent (though still fallible) policies, particularly in relation to child protection. (See, for example, Hester, Pearson and Harwin 2000.)

What seems striking, however, is the fact that, despite the improvements in policy and awareness, women still experience considerable inconsistency in their dealings with representatives of the social work and criminal justice systems. Women are vulnerable not only to the danger and fear of the violence and abuse itself, but also because they cannot rely on protection from police and courts, and still fear the intrusion of social workers. It is still very much the case that most social work activity occurs with the woman as the primary conduit of family business and that men themselves are not held accountable or brought into the picture as far as their violence against partners and children is concerned.

It is only when violence becomes the concern of courts that men tend to be brought to account, and even then traditional court responses suggest that women's position may be further imperilled.

Violence and the Courts

Those responsible for both prosecution and sentencing have commented on what they see as inherent difficulties in processing domestic violence cases. When men's programmes were being set up in Scotland several sentencers stated that they would prefer either to adopt diversionary procedures or to operate under civil proceedings, such as the Matrimonial Homes Act 1983 in England and Wales and the Matrimonial Homes (Family Protection) (Scotland) Act 1981. They saw these as the major vehicles for increased civil protection for women victims of violence (Morran 1996).

In dealing with domestic violence as criminal cases, prosecutors and sentencers referred to the complexity in many instances of the victim's loyalty to the accused, and the pressures on women over time to change their accounts, resulting in perpetuating court prejudices that domestic violence victims are intrinsically unreliable as witnesses and such cases difficult to process

(Moody and Tombs 1982). Sentencers also expressed considerable frustration that many of the sanctions open to them, such as monetary fines or (usually short) custodial sentences, impacted negatively on the victim as well as the perpetrator, perhaps even more so (Morran 1996). The question then put to sentencers was, if, for example, a fine on the perpetrator impacts on the income of the victim, or if a custodial sentence merely makes things worse for the woman on the man's release, whether it was possible to employ a sanction which focuses simultaneously on the man's responsibility for his violence and on the needs and wishes of the victim. It was argued that the work of programmes for violent men, which we discuss below, while not without its share of ethical dilemmas, went further than most other responses to meeting both these aims. Gradually a number of sentencers were won over.

Men's programmes: holding men responsible

Before looking in more detail at how men's programmes try to address these objectives it is necessary to comment on how the problem of 'battered wives' came to be re-framed as the problem of 'male violence against women'.

Throughout the 1980s feminist analyses of 'domestic violence' relocated 'men's violence against wives' not in the dysfunctional pathologies of individual men (and women!), nor as a systemic problem within particular families or sectors of society (read working class), but instead as behaviour which was essentially functional, rooted in patriarchal beliefs about women's 'place', and was condoned by the law and by religion. Violence was about the maintenance of control rather than the loss of control so often cited by men when (rarely) they were called to account for their violent behaviour (Dobash and Dobash 1979, 1992; Sonkin *et al.* 1985; Yllo and Bograd 1988).

This perception of violence as intentional behaviour perpetrated most commonly by men against women and, of course, children, found expression in social action, and in campaigning to condemn the violence as essentially criminal and worthy of public condemnation and sanction. As men came to be seen as the problem, so too were classic criminological positions adopted as to whether or not the problem of men's violent offending against partners was to be addressed by punishment, treatment, or other means. Dobash and Dobash (1992) provide a fascinating account of how in the USA during the 1980s debates raged among women's activists who had led the campaigns against men's violence, and among men involved in the emerging men's movement about how to respond to this unfolding epidemic of violence and abuse. Within the fertile therapeutic culture of the USA, treatment programmes for violent men came to the forefront of the debate (a debate now current within the UK). Some hope seemed to be held out in the form of programmes demanded for (appropriately assessed) violent men. The evidence, which was influential in shaping the developing programmes which exist in the UK today, suggested that the most effective interventions would embrace a feminist perspective on men's violence, hold men accountable for their actions, deal with them as 'perpetrators' rather than misunderstood victims, and ideally would operate within a criminal justice (i.e. probation) framework. Programmes would also be accountable in their practice to women's groups (such as Women's Aid in the UK) and to the individual safety and wishes of the women partners of the men concerned (Adams 1988; Edleson and Eisikovits 1985; Hart 1988; Edleson and Syers 1989).

While the debate about the effectiveness of men's programmes still continues, it was clear that nothing else 'worked' as far as sanctions were concerned. Nothing appeared to change men, nor take into account the many and conflicting pressures on the women affected.

It was against this backdrop that the first criminal justice-based men's programmes in the UK were set up in Scotland: Change in Stirling in 1989, (see Morran and Wilson 1994) and the Domestic Violence Probation Project (DVPP) in Edinburgh in 1990. The following account of DVPP illustrates how practice went on to be developed from some of the debates outlined above.

The Edinburgh Domestic Violence Probation Project: background

DVPP was set up in 1990 following a debate within Lothian Regional Council over the appropriateness of including domestic violence cases in a recently established 'diversion from prosecution' scheme. Women's Committee members argued strongly that any sanction which diverted domestic violence cases from prosecution (where sufficient evidence existed to allow for prosecution) gave a negative message to women who had been abused and an ambivalent one to abusers about the seriousness of their violent behaviour. (This debate continues.) Having insisted that the diversion scheme should not consider domestic violence cases, the council set up DVPP to provide a constructive, non-custodial disposal which courts could use following conviction. The logic of working with perpetrators of domestic violence through the criminal courts is that it should increase the safety of women and children in ways that both straightforward punishment disposals and welfare disposals are unlikely to achieve.

Consulting women from assessment to conclusion

Although it is clear that the criminal justice system is the proper arena for domestic violence, the system, as has been argued above, has not always served domestic violence victims well. Because of the continuing, often close, proximity of perpetrator and victim, both the benefits of processing and dealing with men's violence through the criminal courts, and the costs of not doing so, or doing so in a way which does not adequately consider the woman's interests, can be magnified. There is clearly a danger that the 'disempowering' process evident in women's encounters with many agencies, as suggested above, can be continued and reinforced when the man's violence is brought into the criminal justice arena.

Research has shown that on average there will have been 35 assaults on a woman before she first calls the police (Dobash and Dobash 1992). From our experience of consulting women partners in Edinburgh DVPP we also know that despite significant improvements in police practice over the past ten years, a substantial proportion of those cases where the police are called will not result in the man's arrest. In cases where the man is arrested and charged women often report a lack of understanding and information about what happens when he appears in court. Why was he not remanded in custody?

Why *was* he remanded in custody? Is he allowed to appeal against the remand in custody? What do the bail conditions mean? What if I want to see him? Is he allowed to come back to the house to collect his belongings? Why was I not consulted or at least informed about bail conditions?

The process by which defence agents and procurators fiscal negotiate over pleas can also leave women feeling powerless. When the case comes to court, often months after the event, and the woman is present, either as witness in a trial or because the man's lawyer has encouraged him to ensure her presence in court in order to strengthen the plea of mitigation, she will often have to listen to a distorted version of events and have her sense of powerlessness confirmed. She may hear the same rationalisation, minimisation, denial and blame (involving criticism of her) which her partner routinely employs, being repeated, unchallenged, by a lawyer in a public court. When it comes to sentence, there may be a fine imposed which she knows she will end up paying herself, a non-custodial disposal which she does not understand and which has no relevance to the offence, or a custodial sentence which, although it may contribute to her safety and allow her to enact her safety plan, may leave her feeling deserted and very afraid about her partner's response on his release.

Because of the many obstacles inherent in the system and the often intense pressures put on women to withdraw allegations, an assault allegation which clears each hurdle in the criminal justice process and results in a conviction is often a particularly significant one for women. This might be because of its seriousness, or perhaps because it was witnessed by the children, or perhaps because it represented a situation which the woman was seeing as 'the final straw'. The following statements that women have made to workers in Edinburgh DVPP describe the significance of the assault in question and suggest how important it was for them that the court system respond appropriately.

> I spent my childhood watching my father hit my mother. When I married I told my husband if he hit me, I would get the police. This is the first time this man has ever hit me and it was important for me that I told police.

If my neighbour hadn't come when she did, I know I would have died. At first he was charged with assault to severe injury. It's now down to common assault, but he and I both know he was trying to murder me.

He's told me for years that the police would only laugh at a big woman like me saying I have been assaulted by him, and for years I believed him.

It is at the pre-sentence stage that the project may be asked by the court to assess the man's suitability for participation in the programme. As an integral part of this assessment process DVPP has now consulted over 400 women partners of men convicted of domestic violence offences. The process for consulting women was developed with the advice of local Women's Aid groups. The aim is to get an accurate picture of the man's abuse and the risk which he represents, and to seek the woman's co-operation in monitoring the man's behaviour while he is subject to the probation order. During our first assessment interview with the offender he is informed that DVPP will be attempting to make contact with his partner or ex-partner, and also that no other information will be given to him directly about that contact.

DVPP is clear that only by listening to women can we gain an accurate picture of the current offence and how it fits with any previous pattern of behaviour. As such this consultation process is essential in order for us to work effectively with the man. Women are asked to complete a behaviour checklist which catalogues types and frequency of 'tactics of control' (see Pence and Paymar 1990) that have been used against them. In asking a woman to place the current offence in the context of past abuse in this way we invite her to consider other tactics of control that he may have used and which are not in themselves criminal. This can be distressing for many women especially if, for whatever reason, they have previously attempted to minimise the extent of the man's behaviour. It is vital that we believe what women say because some of the abuse experienced by women can be so extreme, or perhaps bizarre in nature, that women's reluctance to report it can often be partly owing to the fact that it appears so unbelievable. It is also vital because women often report that this is the first opportunity they have had to tell someone within the criminal justice process about the extent of the abuse, without having to corroborate each individual act with physical evidence. This interview is also an opportunity to give factual information to a woman who perhaps has never previously reported the abuse. She may be using this period when her husband is remanded in custody or bailed not to approach her, to make plans to reconsider the relationship.

The issue of the woman's degree of control over the process of consultation and the report which results from it is crucial both for her safety and for her sense of empowerment. Some women will tell their partners that they have refused to speak to DVPP, when in fact they have made contact in secret. Because the defendant and his lawyer always receive copies of DVPP reports, it is made plain to women that any information they give during the interview will be included in the report only with their permission. Sometimes a woman, after discussing and thinking through the implications for her own safety, will say that she wants a full account of the interview conveyed to the sentencing sheriff. In most cases, however, the report will state that the partner has been consulted, but make no direct reference to her statements.

If the woman has decided that no reference should be made to her interview but is anxious that the court should be aware of her partner's previous abuse, we will seek alternative sources of the information. In Edinburgh, DVPP uses the information gathered by police Domestic Violence Liaison Officers to lay before the court – for example, the number of previous callouts to the perpetrator's address. Even if the woman does not wish reference to be made to her statements in the court report, her information will have added to the knowledge of workers and will have influenced them in their recommendations.

Consulting women post sentence

Following sentence, DVPP asks the partners of men who are required to attend the programme to act as consultants throughout the life of the order – whether or not they continue to live with the man. The men understand that this is a condition of their probation order. During the order, workers ask to meet the woman on two or three occasions throughout the first 12-month period, generally prior to each probation review, and ask her to comment on the man's continuing behaviour. In addition to these scheduled contacts women are encouraged to remain in regular telephone contact with information about the man's behaviour. Again, this information is always treated confidentially. In building this relationship with women DVPP is explicitly making the shift from seeing them as victims to treating them as consultants and experts on their partner's behaviour.

The format and purpose of the post-sentence consultation interviews is different from that of those undertaken during the assessment stage. We decided that in cases where the man is undertaking the programme, we need to know more than whether he is continuing to use specific forms of abusive behaviour or not. We need to seek feedback from women partners on any positive change, marked by an increased commitment by the man to a positive and constructive model of intimate relationships, rather than simply the absence of abusive behaviour.

Personal construct theory

In order to do this we borrowed the concept of bi-polar constructs from personal construct theory (see Kelly 1963) and developed a series of constructs which we present as scales or continuums on eight different aspects of behaviour, based broadly on the dichotomy between relationships based on power and control and those based on equality (Pence and Paymar 1990).

| **Putting you down, calling you names, etc.** | **Valuing your opinions, listening with respect** |

$$-3 -2 -1 \ 0 +1 +2 +3$$

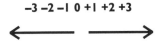

In conducting partner interviews both at the post-sentence stage and towards the end of the programme we ask the woman to score her partner's behaviour somewhere between +3 (at the 'equality' end of the continuum) and −3 (at the 'power and control' end) for each construct. In developing this tool we were conscious of the fact that it also measures behaviour rather than attitude, and we know that long-term behaviour change only comes about with attitude change. The second part of the interview schedule therefore involves an attempt to elicit from the woman a series of constructs which would serve as a realistic benchmark for measuring her partner's attitude. We ask her to put into her own words what she would like her partner's attitude to be, such that, if he made the shift towards it, would lead her to assume an increase in her safety and freedom. We then ask her to name the polar opposite, negative, attitudes. She might come up with constructs such as 'possessive' versus 'trusts me' or 'treats me like his mother' *versus* 'treats me like an equal'. Using these newly elicited bi-polar constructs, the woman can score her partner's attitude at different stages of his involvement in the programme, to help her and us measure the changes he may be making (see the following example).

possessive   **trusts me**

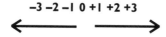

−3 −2 −1 0 +1 +2 +3

DVPP has found this format for consulting partners helpful. The very struc-tured form of listening more genuinely takes into account the individual woman's reality, and the process can help her in her safety planning by en-couraging her to evaluate the changes which her partner may be making. It may also enable her to differentiate between those changes made because of the threat of sanctions and those changes which arise from a genuine shift in attitude. We also believe that the process can be empowering because it invites a woman who is scared and controlled in her behaviour and in her verbalising of her situation to construe and possibly reconstrue the situation. We should stress that any positive benefits of using this approach to structure consultation depend entirely upon the existence of proper procedures for ensuring the safety and confidentiality of those being consulted. (For a fuller discussion of the use of personal construct theory in men's programme work, see Macrae and Andrew 1999).

It has long been recognised in this field that an absolute minimum standard for perpetrator work is that each project should have well-established and safe mechanisms for confidentially consulting women's partners, one model of which we have described above. In order to ensure that the work with men is done non-collusively and in a victim-focused way it is essential not only to have 'increasing the safety of women and children' as the primary aim of such work, but also to allow the programme to be shaped and influenced by women who have experienced abuse. We have concentrated in this chapter only on the consultative procedures which ensure that this process happens, and have not examined the role of the DVPP Partner Support Worker whose remit is to work exclusively and proactively with women partners. Best practice requires that perpetrator programmes do provide integrated women's support services (Burton *et al.* 1998; RESPECT 2000).

Victim-focused work with men in the programme

For men who participate in programmes like CHANGE or DVPP it is made clear at the outset that the violence they have used is not something abstract. The man has used this behaviour in particular contexts against his partner or ex-partner and he will be required to discuss his violence and the consequences for his partner as a condition of attending the programme. He must also always refer to his partner by her first name in order to bring home more fully that his behaviour has impacted on a person.

Men invariably find discussing the effects of their violence and abuse very difficult. In the past they have been allowed to deny their violence, blame it on the other party or simply dismiss it either as nothing, 'just a slap', or as something outside their control: 'I just saw red!' Now the man is required to look afresh at the physical and psychological impact of his behaviour on the woman (who may still live with him) and to consider the consequences for their relationship and for other family members, particularly children.

As research into effectiveness of offender programmes generally has observed, the fact that the victim perspective is taken into consideration can be a core element of positive behaviour change (Scottish Office 1991). Among the many changes which men are expected to make during participation in the challenging environment of men's programmes is that they gradually come to see their partner as a person and not as an object. As the programmes have developed, and taking into account recent research (Hester *et al.* 2000), we have, in addition to focusing on the impact of the violence on women, increasingly taken into consideration the effects of violence on children. The authors argued at the beginning of this chapter that traditional social work responses to domestic violence were focused almost entirely on children, to the exclusion or detriment of women. We would suggest that our work represents a significant shift in that it takes into account the impact of violence on children but now holds men clearly accountable for their violence and its effects on both their partners and children alike.

Recent research into the UK men's programmes (CHANGE and Edinburgh DVPP) has indicated that men who participated, in contrast to those who experience other forms of criminal justice sanctions such as fines, probation or imprisonment, successfully reduced their violent and controlling behaviour (over a one-year period). The comments of both men and women pointed to a reduction of the level and frequency of violence. Significantly, comments also referred to changes in the ways in which men thought about their violence and about their partners (Dobash *et al.* 1996).

An innovative measure introduced into this study was a scale whereby men and women discussed 'quality of life' during and after the various sanctions. The researchers concluded that '… a significant proportion of women in the Programme group report(ed) that twelve months after (first) interview, their partners are more likely to see their point of view, to be aware of their feelings, to respect them, to be more sympathetic and less self-centred'. In comparison: 'Only a small proportion of women in the other (Criminal Justice sanctions) group report positive changes in these areas and many report a deterioration' (Dobash *et al.* 1996, vii).

Conclusion

Violent men's programmes thus allow men to change by providing a framework which other sanctions do not offer. In contrast to monetary or punishment-based disposals, for example, they allow men to realise that change is possible, that the man can think beyond himself and begin to include others, i.e. his partner/victim, in his thinking. Comments by the research team again describe this process succinctly:

> The majority of men in the other CJ group seem almost completely untouched by any 'new' notions about their violence, responsibility, notions of blameworthiness and their need for change…Programme men have replaced their old language with an alternative discourse reflecting new notions about women, partners, themselves, and their violence which expands the cognitive and emotional landscape to include greater reflection by the men upon their past, present and future. (*ibid.* ix)

Since 1991 those working with perpetrators of domestic violence have been involved in a UK-wide practitioners' network which meets regularly to share and develop good and accountable practice. Over the course of that time a statement of principles and minimum standards for ethical practice has been drawn up (see RESPECT 2000).

As practitioners committed to the standards espoused by RESPECT, we would suggest that the work of the programmes discussed here is victim-focused from the point of assessment to completion, and that more than any other criminal justice sanction the issue of the woman's safety is addressed throughout, her 'expertise' in the matter of the violence to which she has been subjected is respected, and, should she wish to offer it, her consultancy is both highly valued and highly valuable to programme workers.

Note:

Moira Andrew and Rory Macrae can be contacted at:
The City of Edinburgh Domestic Violence Probation Project
21 Market Street, Edinburgh EH1 1BL
Tel. 0131 469 3401

References

Adams D. (1988) 'Treatment models of men who batter: A pro-feminist analysis.' In K. Yllo and M. Bograd (eds.) *Feminist Perspectives on Wife Abuse*. London: Sage.

Binney V., Harkill, G. and Noon, J. (1985) 'Refuges and housing for battered women.' in J. Dahl (ed.) *Private Violence and Public Policy*. London: Routledge and Kegan Paul.

Borkowski M., Murch M. and Walker V. (1983) *Marital Violence: The Community Reponse*. London and New York: Tavistock.

Bowker L. H. (1983) *Beating Wife Beating*. Lexington, Mass.: Lexington Books.

Bruce E. (1979) 'Attitudes of social workers and police in the Select Committee reports on violence to women and children.' In J. Hanmer (ed.) *Battered Women and Abused Children (Intricacies of Legal and Administrative Intervention)*. Issues Occasional Paper No. 4.

Burton S., Regan L. and Kelly L. (1998) *Challenging Men: Lessons from the Domestic Violence Intervention Project*. Policy Press in association with the Joseph Rowntree Foundation.

Dobash R. E. and Dobash R. P. (1979) *Violence Against Wives*. New York: Free Press.

Dobash R. E. and Dobash R. P. (1992) *Women, Violence and Social Change*. London: Routlege and Kegan Paul.

Dobash R. E., Dobash R. P. and Cavanagh K. (1985) 'The contact between battered women and social and medical agencies.' In J. Pahl (ed.) *Private Violence and Public Policy*. London: Routledge and Kegan Paul.

Dobash R. E., Dobash R. P., Kavanagah K. and Lewis R. (1996) *Research Evaluation of Programmes for Violent Men*. Edinburgh: The Scottish Office Central Research Unit.

Edleson J. L. and Eisikovits Z. (1985) 'Men who batter women: A critical view of the evidence.' *Journal of Family Issues* 6, 2, June, 229–247.

Edleson J. L. and Syers M. (1989) *The Relative Effectiveness of Group Treatment for Men who Batter*. Minneapolis, MN: Domestic Abuse Project.

Gagnon C. and Lavoie F. (1990) 'The attitude of social service intervenors toward women abused by partners and their feeling of competence.' *Canadian Social Work Review* 7, 2, summer, 197–214.

Gayford J. J. (1975) 'Wife battering: a preliminary survey of 100 cases. *British Medical Journal*, January, 194–197.

Gayford J. J. (1976) 'Ten types of battered wives.' *Welfare Officer* 25, 1, 5–9.

Hanmer J. and Leonard D. (1984) 'Negotiating the problem: The DHSS and research and violence in marriage.' In C. Bell and H. Roberts (eds.) *Social Researching: Politics, Problems, Practice*. London: Routledge and Kegan Paul.

Hart B. (1988) *Safety for Women: Monitoring Batterers Programs*. Harrisburg PA: Pennsylvania Coalition Against Domestic Violence.

Hester M., Pearson C. and Harwin N. (2000) *Making an Impact: Children and Domestic Violence: A Reader*. London: Jessica Kingsley.

Kelly G. A. (1963) *A Theory of Personality: The Psychology of Personal Constructs*. New York: Norton.

Macrae R. and Andrew M. (2000) 'The use of personal construct theory in work with men who abuse women partners.' *Probation Journal* 47, 1, 30–38.

Maynard M. (1985) 'The response of social workers to domestic violence.' In J. Pahl (ed.) *Private Violence and Public Policy*. London: Routledge and Kegan Paul.

Moody S. R. and Tombs J. (1982) *Prosecutions in the Public Interest*. Edinburgh: Scottish Academic Press.

Morran D. (1996) 'Working with male domestic violence offenders.' In G. Mair and T. Newburn (eds.) *Work with Men.* Lyme Regis: Russell House.

Morran D. and Wilson,M. (1994) 'Confronting domestic violence: An innovative criminal justice response in Scotland.' In A. Duff, S. Marshall, R. E. Dobash and R. P. Dobash (eds.) *Penal Theory and Practice: Tradition and Innovation in Criminal Justice.* Manchester University Press in association with the Fulbight Commission, London.

Pahl J. (1981) *A Bridge Over Troubled Waters: A Longitudinal Study of Women who Went to a Refuge.* Report to DHSS.

Pahl J. (ed.) (1985) *Private Violence and Public Policy: The Needs of Battered Women and the Response of Public Services.* London: Routledge and Kegan Paul.

Pence E. and Paymar M. (1990) *Power and Control: Tactics of Men Who Batter.* Duluth, MN: Minnesota Program Development Inc., Duluth.

Pizzey E. (1974) *Scream Quietly or the Neighbours Will Hear.* Harmondsworth: Penguin.

RESPECT (2) *The Statement of Principles and Good Practice Guidelines.* Available from DVIP PO Box 2836. Hammersmith, London W69ZE.

Sankin, J.S., Martin, D. and Walker, L.E.A. (1985) *The Male Batterer – A Treatment Approach.* New York: Springer.

Schlesinger P., Dobash R. E, Dobash R. P. and Weaver C. K. (1992) *Women Viewing Violence.* London: British Film Institute.

Scottish Home and Health Department (Edinburgh) (1990) *Police (CC) Circular No. 3/1990: Investigation of Complaints of Domestic Assault.*

Select Committee Report (1975) *Violence in Marriage,* HCP 553,II. London: HMSO.

Smith L. (1989) 'Domestic Violence.' Home Office Research Study No. 107. London: HMSO.

Social Work Services Group (1991) *National Objectives and Standards for Social Work Services in the Criminal Justice System.* Edinburgh: The Scottish Office.

Wilson E. (1983) *What is to be Done About Violence Against Women?* Harmondsworth: Penguin.

Yllo K. and Bograd M. (1988) *Feminist Perspectives on Wife Abuse.* London and New York: Sage.

The contributors

Moira Andrew is an experienced criminal justice social worker. She has worked on the Domestic Violence Probation Programme in Edinburgh, Scotland, since its inception in 1990, and helped to design the programme. With Rory Macrae, she is involved in providing training and consultancy to other projects.

Karen Chouhan is the Director of the 1990 Trust (a national black, non-governmental organisation), on secondment from her post as senior lecturer in community education at De Montfort University, Leicester, England. She is the managing director of the Race and Ethnic Diversity Research and Policy Partnership (REDRAPP) and also manages the Black Studies Unit. She specialises in training, programmes, policy development, anti-discriminatory practice and managing diversity, particularly in partnership between academia and black communities. She has worked on this with partner organisations in Germany, France and the Netherlands. She prepared an independent report on the Stephen Lawrence Inquiry entitled *A Culture of Denial*, and remains involved in influencing the direction of anti-racist work after the Inquiry.

Jim Dignan, LL.B., M.A., is a Reader at the Centre for Criminological and Legal Research at the University of Sheffield, England. He has written on a variety of theoretical, practical and policy-related issues raised by the development of restorative justice, and was a member of the team commissioned by the Home Office to evaluate the pilot Youth Offending Teams and the youth justice reforms introduced by the Crime and Disorder Act 1998.

Jane Dominey works as a probation officer in Cambridgeshire, England. Over the past ten years she has practised in a number of settings, including community supervision, groupwork and resettlement. At present she is a practice development assessor, responsible for the teaching and training of trainee probation officers. She has been particularly involved in training in the areas of ethical practice and probation work with victims of crime.

Jo Goodey received her PhD from the University of Hull in 1995. Since then she has worked as a criminology lecturer in northern England at the Universities of Sheffield and Leeds. She is currently on a two-year sabbatical from the Centre for Criminal Justice Studies at The University of Leeds, and is based as a research fellow at the Centre for International Crime Prevention at the United Nations in Vienna, Austria. The European Commission funds her research into criminal justice responses to vulnerable and at-risk victims in the European Union, including the treatment of women who are trafficked into Europe for enslavement in the sex industry. She is broadly interested in victim-centred research and has published widely in this area, including *Integrating a Victim Perspective within Criminal Justice: International Debates* co-edited with Adam Crawford.

Charlotte Knight is principal lecturer in Community and Criminal Justice at De Montfort University, Leicester, England. She is programme leader for the BA (Hons) degree in Community and Criminal Justice, which leads to the professional qualification in probation practice. This programme highlights issues of racism within the criminal justice system and its impact on workers, offenders and victims. She previously worked as a probation officer and a senior probation officer in Leicestershire. Her interest in victims stems from development work with community service orders, including an element of reparative work on the houses of burglary victims. More recently she has worked with Leicester Mediation Service to raise awareness of victim–offender mediation schemes.

Guy Masters completed his PhD in criminology in 1997 and has been working in the field of restorative justice since 1993. He has undertaken research about family group conferencing, restorative conferencing, victim–offender mediation and family mediation in a number of countries and is currently a member of the team evaluating the piloting of referral orders in England and Wales. While senior consultant with Crime Concern he provided support and training in restorative practice for several Youth Offending Teams, wrote national guidance notes on effective restorative practice for the Youth Justice Board, and helped develop a mediation and reparation service in partnership with Wessex Youth Offending Team. Guy is currently a post-doctoral research fellow at the centre for Restorative Justice, Australian National University.

Rory Macrae is an experienced criminal justice social worker. He has worked in the Domestic Violence Probation Programme in Edinburgh, Scotland, since 1992. He took part in an exchange programme with a men's domestic violence programme in Australia for six months in 1998. With Moira Andrew, he is involved in providing training and consultancy to other projects.

David Morran is a lecturer in social work at the University of Stirling, Scotland, and has written and taught on issues related to male violence in relationships. He was previously joint co-ordinator of the CHANGE men's programme in Stirling. Prior to that he worked in a men's prison, where he became increasingly interested in masculinity and crime. His first post was as a generic social worker in Glasgow, and he has also worked as a development officer for SACRO, the Scottish Association for the Care and Resettlement of Offenders.

Susan R. Moody is a senior lecturer in law at the University of Dundee. Her main research areas are crime victims and legal issues relating to volunteering. She was formerly director of Victim Support Scotland and is active in Scottish initiatives concerned with victims, and work with offenders. She is currently carrying out a study of racist victimisation and the impact of new offences of racially aggravated crime in Scotland for the Scottish Executive. She is a member of the Scientific Committee of the International Society of Criminology.

Barbara Tudor has worked as a social worker with older people, people with visual impairments, people with learning difficulties, in adoption, and as a signer between hearing teachers and profoundly deaf students. She was appointed as a mediator for West Midlands Probation Service in Coventry, England, 1985, in one of the Home Office Reparation Scheme Pilots subsequently becoming its manager. In 1996 she became the service's Victim–Offender Development Officer with a development, training, monitoring and evaluation remit within the West Midlands and further afield. She has personal experience of over 3500 victim–offender mediation cases from caution to post-release stages.

Sandra Walklate is Professor of Sociology at Manchester Metropolitan University in England. She has written extensively about criminal victimisation, the fear of crime, and policing. Since the early 1980s she has worked with different victim support organisations, both as a volunteer and as a training consultant. She is currently working on a book on murder for Willan Publishing.

Dr Jo-Anne Wemmers is Assistant Professor in the School of Criminology at the University of Montréal, Canada, and is a principal researcher at the International Centre for Comparative Criminology. She has published widely on victim issues and restorative justice practices. She has contributed to the development of the *UN Manual* and *Handbook on Basic Principles of Justice for Victims of Crime and Abuse of Power* and is a member of the International Advisory Board for the International Victimology Website, hosted by the Ministry of Justice of the Netherlands in affiliation with the United Nations and the World Society of Victimology. She is managing editor of *The Victimologist*, the newsletter of the World Society of Victimology.

Dr Brian Williams is Reader in Criminal Justice at De Montfort University, Leicester, England. He previously worked as a probation officer and as a lecturer at Teesside, Sheffield and Keele universities. He has published widely in his main areas of research, which include professionals' work with victims of crime, and inter-agency responses to youth offending. He is a member of the Council of the British Society of Criminology, and secretary of its ethics panel.

Subject Index

Author Index